Paul McCartney

Printed in the United Kingdom by MPG Books Ltd, Bodmin

Published by Sanctuary Publishing Limited, Sanctuary House, 45–53 Sinclair Road,
London W14 0NS, United Kingdom

www.sanctuarypublishing.com

Distributed in the US by Publishers Group West

ISBN: 1-86074-520-2

Paul McCartney

Alan Clayson
Sanctuary

Contents

1 "Que Sera Sera"

When, in the first flush of their stardom, The Beatles made their stage debut in Ireland – at Dublin's Adelphi Cinema on 7 November 1963 – Paul McCartney announced that "It's great to be home!". Liverpool, see, is known facetiously as "the capital of Ireland" – and three of the Moptopped Mersey Marvels had more than a splash of the Auld Sod in their veins.

Most of Paul's was inherited from mother Mary, whose maiden name was Mohin. Almost as a matter of course, she was devoutly Roman Catholic. Yet, while she kept the pledge required of the Catholic party in such a union to have any offspring baptised into the faith, her two sons – James Paul and Peter Michael – were not to be educated in Roman Catholic schools or to attend Roman Catholic churches, which stood in Merseyside suburbs becoming lost in an encroaching urban sprawl that had spread from central Liverpool since The Great War when 14-year-old Jim McCartney had entered the world of work on the ground floor at a dockside cotton merchant's. He'd risen to the high office of salesman there by the next global conflict when, as an infinitesimal cog provisioning the bloodshed afar, he did his bit in a local munitions factory. Then, following Hitler's suicide, Jim passed a written test for eligibility to work for Liverpool Corporation. He was introduced to Mary Mohin by one of his sisters and married her in 1941.

Just over a year later, the remarkable James Paul was born on 18 June 1942, a dry Thursday with alternate warm and cool spells, in Liverpool's Walton Hospital, the nearest maternity ward to the furnished rooms in Anfield where Jim and Mary lived in a forlorn cluster of Coronation Streets.

The "James" was both after his father and in respect of the scriptures, but, from the cradle, the boy was called by his middle name, just as his brother – who arrived two years later – was to be.

From Anfield, the family moved to the south of Liverpool, settling eventually in 20 Forthlin Road, a semi-detached on a new estate in Allerton, ten minutes dawdle from the river, and more convenient for Mrs McCartney in her capacity as health visitor and then a district midwife.

In the living room stood an upright piano. Whilst it suffered the investigative pounding of the infant Paul and Mike's plump fists, it also tinkled beneath the self-taught hands of their father who, in the 1920s, had had no qualms about performing in public, whether extrapolating often witty incidental music as silent movies flickered in city cinemas or performing at parochial entertainments on the 88s – and, for a while, trumpet – with his Jim Mac's Jazz Band.

Obliged by economic necessity to focus more exclusively on his day job, Jim cut back on the extra-curricular Charlestons, finally breaking up the band, circa 1927. Nevertheless, he continued to play for his own amusement and compose too, though the only extant Jim McCartney opus seems to be 'Walking In The Park With Eloise', an instrumental.

Sensibly, while Jim was only too willing to impart hard-won knowledge, neither he nor Mary goaded their lads to over-formalise what were assumed to be innate musical strengths. Of the two, Paul seemed keenest and, from being a fascinated listener whenever Dad was seated at the piano, progressed at his own speed on the instrument, acquiring the rudiments of harmony, and adding to a repertoire that embraced tunes from cross-legged primary school assemblies and – then quite a new idea – traditional songs from *Singing Together* and other BBC Home Service radio broadcasts to schools.

More exciting than the Home Service's dashing white sergeants, drunken sailors, Li'l Liza Janes and John Barleycorniness was the Light Programme, which interspersed the likes of Educating Archie – comic goings-on of a ventriloquist's dummy (on the radio!) – and *Workers' Playtime* with approved items from the newly established *New Musical Express* record sales "hit parade".

Like all but the most stuffy adolescents of the 1950s, Paul McCartney would be thrilled by 'Rock Around The Clock' whenever it intruded upon the Light Programme's jingle bells and winter wonderlands as 1955 drew to a close. But as he later explained, "the first time I really ever felt a tingle up my spine was when I saw Bill Haley And The Comets playing it on the telly."

Now a loose-lipped and rather chubby youth, Paul had left Joseph Williams Primary School, a "bus ride away from Forthlin Road, after passing the Eleven-Plus examination to gain a place at Liverpool Institute, which was located within the clang of bells from both the Roman Catholic and Anglican cathedrals, along with most of the city centre's other seats of learning, including the university – opened in 1978 on the site of the old lunatic asylum – and the Regional College of Art.

Thus far, Paul had proved sound enough, even very able, in most subjects. He had a particular flair and liking for creative writing because as well as submitting homework, he would tinker with fragments of verse and prose for a purpose unknown apart from articulating the inner space of some private cosmos.

It goes without saying that he shone during music lessons too. Indeed, while he'd never be able to sight-read faster than the most funereal pace, he became as well-known for his musical skills as the school bully and football captain were in their chosen spheres. However, an attempt to master a second-hand trumpet his father had given him was, let's say, an "incomplete success", put off as he was by the unpredictable harmonics, which jarred his teeth during his first shaky sessions in front of a prescribed manual. "Guitars hadn't come in yet," he'd recall. "Trumpeters were the big heroes then." Eddie Calvert, Britain's foremost trumpeter, was from Preston in the same neck of the wood as Liverpool. If well into his 30s, he'd shown what was possible by scoring a 1954 Number One in the *New Musical Express*'s chart with sentimental 'Oh Mein Papa', recorded at EMI's studio complex along Abbey Road, a stone's throw from Lord's Cricket Ground in far-away London.

Eddie's renown was to infiltrate a Giles cartoon in the *Daily Express* in which an elderly classical musician with a trumpet under his arm is mobbed for autographs by teenagers at the Edinburgh Festival. Three other members of the orchestra watch the frenzy ill-humouredly. "How does he do it?" rhetoricates a cellist. "Signs himself Eddie Calvert. That's how he does it."

How could any British musician become more famous than to be the inspiration for Carl Giles? Young Paul McCartney was impressed, "but I couldn't sing with a trumpet, and I wanted to sing." This wish was granted after a fashion because Paul's musical genesis was ecclesiastic as well as academic, and his then unbroken soprano was put to use in the choir at St Barnabas Church, off Penny Lane, common ground between the raw red council houses of Allerton and, half a class up, the mock-Tudor thoroughfares of Woolton, a suburb that regarded itself as more "county" than "city".

In cassock, ruff and surplice, Paul cantillated at three services every Sunday and, when required, at weddings and in St Cecilia's Day oratorios. Then, in 1953, with hardly a murmur, he had gone along with his father's advice to try for Liverpool's Anglican Cathedral choir. Another supplicant was John Charles Duff Lowe, a boy who was to be in the same class as Paul at the Institute. In middle life, Lowe came upon "a photograph taken when Paul and I both auditioned for the Liverpool Cathedral choir when we were ten, just before we went to the Institute. We both failed on that occasion. I got in six months later, but Paul never tried again. I think he was recorded as saying he'd tried to make his voice break because he didn't really want to do it. "

Whatever Jim's thwarted aspirations for Paul as perhaps a round-vowelled solo tenor setting the Cathedral walls a-tremble with one of Handel's biblical arias, his wife imagined Paul as either a teacher or a doctor. She was, however, never to see either of her children grown to man's estate because, during the summer of 1955, 47-year-old Mary had the removed look of a dying woman – which she was. What she may have self-diagnosed as stomach acidity and non-related chest pains turned out to be terminal cancer.

A photograph on the mantelpiece was to prompt opaque memories of life before the end came on 31 October 1956 –

though, in many respects, Mary continued to govern family behaviour patterns from the grave, especially those rooted in appreciation of the value of money, and the notion that hard work and tenacity are principal keys to achievement.

Life without a wife wasn't easy for Jim at first. For a northern male, he was obliged to become unusually attentive to household tasks, particularly cooking. With assistance from relations and neighbours, however, he ensured that his – thankfully, healthy – offspring were as comfortable and contented as his new station as a single parent would allow.

Paul and Mike helped according to their capabilities with jobs on the rotas their father would pin up in the kitchen. Yet though the situation nurtured self-reliance, Paul's childhood was shorter than it needed to be, even as he stayed on at school beyond the statutory age, raised recently to 16. He was a likeable and seemingly unassuming pupil, who walked a tightrope between teacher's pet and the source of illicit and entertaining distraction as some withered pedagogue droned like a bluebottle in a dusty classroom. "Paul was a very amusing cartoonist," laughed John Duff Lowe. "His drawings – maybe one of the master taking the lesson – would appear under your desk, and you'd pass it on."

Before entering the sixth form, Paul had been securely in the "A" stream throughout his sojourn at the Institute, even winning a school prize for an essay. As it was with future Beatle colleagues, Pete Best and Stuart Sutcliffe, distinguishing themselves likewise at Liverpool Collegiate and Prescot

Grammar respectively, teacher training college, rather than medical school, was looming larger as the summer examinations crept closer. Paul, however, wasn't keen, half-fancying the idea of being some sort of bohemian artist. One of the two GCE "A" levels he was expected to pass was actually in Art, a subject that the ordinary working man from the northwest saw as having doubtful practical value. Certainly, no artist based in Liverpool was usually able to rely solely on his work for a reasonable income.

Musicians were in the same boat. If on a business trip to Manchester, "Entertainment Capital of the North", moguls from EMI or the kingdom's other three major record companies rarely seized the chance to sound out talent in Macclesfield, Preston, Liverpool or other conurbations within easy reach. In the realm of pop, it had been necessary for Eddie Calvert to go to the capital to Make It. The same applied to chart-climbing Liverpudlian vocalists like Lita Roza, Michael Holliday – and Frankie Vaughan, who, in 1958, had become a bigger pop star than even Eddie Calvert. There were, nonetheless, perceptible signs of danger for Frankie after the coming of ITV's *Oh Boy!*, a series pitched directly at teenagers.

Oh Boy! arrived a year after Bill Haley's first European tour – the first by any US rock 'n' roller. "The ticket was 24 shillings," remembered Paul, "and I was the only one of my mates who could go as no one else had been able to save that amount – but I was single-minded about it, having got that tingle up my spine. I knew there was something going on here."

Described by *Melody Maker* as resembling a "genial butcher", Haley was an ultimate disappointment at the Liverpool Empire and virtually everywhere else, though he paved the way for more genuine articles.

Paul McCartney had been approaching his 14th birthday when he first caught Elvis Presley's 'Heartbreak Hotel' on the Light Programme. In a then-unimaginable future, he was to own the double-bass thrummed on this 78rpm single, but in 1956, he was just one of countless British youths who'd been so instantly "gone" on 'Heartbreak Hotel' that all he could think was that its maker was surely the greatest man ever to have walked the planet. Listening to this and consequent Presley hits either sent McCartney into a reverie that no one could penetrate or brought on an onset of high spirits that drew in Mike and even a bemused Jim. It was to be the same when he discovered Little Richard. In a typically succinct foreword to Richard's 1984 biography, Paul would recollect, "The first song I ever sang in public was 'Long Tall Sally' in a Butlin's holiday camp talent competition when I was 14."

So "gone" was he this time that he started buying Little Richard discs without first listening to them – as you could in those days – in the shop, thus bringing upon himself angered dismay when "I found this Little Richard album that I'd never seen before. When I played it, I found there were only two tracks by Little Richard. The rest was by Buck Ram and his Orchestra. You needed a magnifying glass to find that out from the sleeve. It's rotten, that kind of thing."

Richard was not to visit Britain until he'd shed the qualificative bulk of his artistic load, but a singing guitarist named Buddy Holly did, leaving a lasting and beneficial impression upon one who was to be his greatest champion. Visually, Holly, unlike Presley, was no romantic lead from a Hollywood flick, recast as a rock 'n' roller. To offset an underfed gawkiness, Buddy wore a huge pair of black horn-rims. Until he and his accompanying Crickets – guitar, bass and drums – played Liverpool's Philharmonic Hall on 20 March 1958, Paul McCartney had been attracted by "really good-looking performers like Elvis. Any fellow with glasses always took them off to play, but after Buddy, anyone who really needed glasses could then come out of the closet."

Yet it was still a magazine picture of a smouldering Elvis on the bedroom wall that greeted Paul when he first opened his eyes in the pallor of dawn. Presley was also hovering metaphorically in the background during Paul's maiden attempts to make romantic contact with girls who, in the years before the contraceptive pill, had been brought up to discourage completion of sexual pilgrimages until their wedding nights.

McCartney, however, was to enjoy more such conquests than most, his appeal emphasised by not infrequent paternity allegations after The Beatles left the runway. Among forums for initiating carnal adventures were coffee bars like the Jacaranda where, according to a regular customer named Rod Jones, "there used to be office girls who'd go up there to get laid because all the art students used to hang around there."

2 "That'll Be The Day"

Paul knew Rod Jones, but not as well as he did one who'd started his art college course a year earlier in 1957. How had Paul classified John Lennon during the first days of their acquaintance? Was he a friend?

To all intents and purposes, Lennon – nearly two years older than McCartney – had lived with his aunt in well-to-do Woolton from infancy. Soon to die, his mother dwelt nearby with his half-siblings and her boyfriend. After she'd gone, John was not to understand the profundity of the less absolute loss of his father until much later. The situation with his parents was a handy peg on which to hang all sorts of frustrations. Life had long ceased to make sense for a very mixed-up kid with a huge chip on his shoulder. From breakfast to bedtime, he projected himself as being hard as nails, as hard as his hardened heart.

Despite everything, Paul – like so many others – couldn't help liking John Lennon. For a start, he was hilarious. His calculated brutishness never quite overshadowed a grace-saving, if sometimes casually shocking, wit as well as a disarming absence of a sense of embarrassment, a selective affability and a fierce loyalty towards those few he'd accepted as intimates.

Something else that interested Paul about John was that he was leader of a "skiffle" group called The Quarry Men. He sang and was one of too many rudimentary guitarists. A chap named Rod Davis picked at a banjo, while the rest used instruments manufactured from household implements.

The skiffle craze had followed a hunt for an innocuous British riposte to Elvis Presley. The job had gone to Tommy Steele, a former merchant seaman, but his first chart strike, 'Rock With The Cavemen', had been shut down in 1956's autumn Top 20 by 'Dead Or Alive' from Lonnie Donegan – 'The King of Skiffle', a form born of the rent parties, speakeasies and Dust Bowl jug bands of the US Depression. Other skiffle stars included Johnny Duncan, a Tennesseean, who came to Britain with the US army, but, awaiting demobilisation, stayed on to cause Lonnie Donegan some nervous backward glances during skiffle's 1957 prime. Johnny drew from the same repertory sources as everyone else – blues, gospel, rockabilly, country et al – but, being a bona fide Yank, he had an edge over the plummy gentility of most native would-be Donegans.

Yet it was Lonnie rather than Johnny who was the dominant precursor of the 1960s beat boom, given those future stars who mastered their assorted crafts in amateur outfits that followed his example. As well as Cliff Richard, Marty Wilde, Adam Faith and others who received more immediate acclaim, Paul McCartney too had taken on skiffle after buying himself an acoustic guitar. Encouraged as he always was by his father, he'd taught himself to play after an initial setback on discovering that he needed to restring it in order to hold down chords commensurate with his left-handedness.

Paul had absorbed pop like blotting paper, and was making what he hoped was a pleasant row on his new acquisition, but Jim would remind him that perhaps it was time to cast aside adolescent follies. He might think that this rock 'n' roll was the most enthralling music ever, but he'd grow out of it. There was no reason why it should last much longer than previous short-lived fads. It just happened to be going a bit stronger than hula-hoops and the cha-cha-cha. Hadn't Paul read in *Melody Maker* that many skiffle musicians were switching their allegiance to less-than-pure traditional jazz, the next big thing, so they said? Unlike skiffle, anyone couldn't do it.

Feeling the chill of reality, Paul sat his GCE "O" levels – two a year early, the remainder during 1958's rainy June. Two months later, the results alighted on the Forthlin Road doormat. Having passed enough to enter the sixth form, he was able to keep that most noxious of human phenomena, a decision about his future, at arm's length for a while longer, enabling the growth of an *idée fixe* that if he kept at it, he might make a reasonable living as a musician.

He didn't know how Jim was going to take any suggestions about a profession that tended to be treated with amused contempt, unless you'd been born to it, but the rising sap of puberty found Paul McCartney seeking openings among suburban music-makers. That's how he'd come to hear of The Quarry Men during the hiatus between "O" and "A" levels. Prospects didn't seem all that bright for them. Engagements beyond Liverpool were unknown, and the line-up was mutable in state, and yet drawn from the same pool of faces. Neither had The Quarry Men yet received actual money for playing when McCartney saw them for the first time at a church fête in Woolton on Saturday, 6 July 1957.

"I noticed this fellow singing with his guitar," said Paul, smiling at the memory, "and he was playing bum chords, and singing 'Come Go With Me' by The Del-Vikings. I realised he was changing the words into folk song and chain gang words, a clever bit of ingenuity. That was Johnny [sic] Lennon. My mate Ivan knew them, so we went backstage, and after a couple of drinks, we were around the piano singing songs to each other. Later, they sort of approached me on a bike somewhere, and said, 'You want to join?'."

From his first date as a Quarry Man – reckoned to be at a Conservative Club functions room on 18 October 1957 – Paul rose quickly through the ranks, coming to rest as

Lennon's lieutenant, and in a position to foist revolutionary doctrines, namely the songs he'd started to write, onto the status quo. The affront to the older boy's superiority was such that Lennon contemplated starting again with new personnel before deciding to try this composing lark himself, and then joining forces with McCartney in what neither of them could even have daydreamed then was to evolve into one of the most outrageously successful songwriting partnerships of all time.

There was no indication of that in 1957. Few, if any, Lennon–McCartney efforts were dared on the boards – probably none at all during slots of three numbers at most in talent contests advertised in the *Echo*, where they'd be up against comedy impressionists, knife-throwers, Shirley Temples and "this woman who played the spoons," glared Paul. "We reckoned we were never going to beat this little old lady as she wiped the floor with us every time. That's when we decided to knock talent contests on the head."

It cost just a little ego-massaging to hire The Quarry Men to do a turn at wedding receptions, youth clubs, parties and "Teenage Shows" offered by cinema proprietors on Saturday mornings – so that Lennon (and McCartney) could enjoy fleeting moments of make-believing they were Donegan or Presley.

As well as a singing voice that was on a par with Lennon's, that McCartney had taken more trouble than the others to learn guitar properly made him one of the group's two natural focal points. Lennon got by less on orthodox ability than force of personality. Moreover, unlike everyone but Paul, he wasn't in it for the sake of his health, but as a purposeful means to make his way as a professional musician.

Not exactly the attraction of opposite as some biographers would have it, John and Paul's liaison was now based as much on amity as shared ambition. Nevertheless, they began weeding out those personnel who either regarded The Quarry Men as no more than a hobby or were just barely proficient passengers who made you flinch whenever you heard a difficult bit coming up in a given song.

Those who got by on home-made instruments were the first to go. Among replacements was John Duff Lowe, who was now a competent rock 'n' roll pianist. Even so, he was subjected to McCartney's quality control. "He asked me to play the introduction to Jerry Lee Lewis's 'Mean Woman Blues'," grinned Lowe. "I did so to his satisfaction, so he invited me to his house in Allerton to meet John Lennon. By then, the repertoire was all Gene Vincent, Buddy Holly, Chuck Berry and so on."

Lowe was present on The Day The Quarry Men Went To A Recording Studio in June 1958. They came away from this suburban Aladdin's cave of reel-to-reel tape machines, editing blocks and jack-to-jack leads with a now-legendary acétate that coupled a pointless replica of 'That'll Be The Day' by Holly's Crickets with 'In Spite Of All The Danger', an original by Paul and 15-year-old lead guitarist George

Harrison, as new a recruit as John Lowe, who affirms that McCartney was the main writer, qualifying this with "Some say that he was inspired by a favourite record of his, 'Tryin' To Get To You' by Elvis Presley, which, when Paul went to Boy Scout camp in 1957, was Number 15 in the UK charts."

The disc was in John Lowe's possession when The Quarry Men faded away sometime in 1959 – though he'd hear that "John and Paul got together again – and George was playing with other groups." As for Lowe himself, "I joined Hobo Rick and his City Slickers, a country-and-western band. I've got a feeling that George played with us on one occasion. It never occurred to me to become a professional musician – though most evenings, I'd be in either a club called the Lowlands or down the Casbah, Pete Best's mother's place."

3 "It's Now Or Never"

Apart from a smattering of offstage lines many acts later, John Duff Lowe's part in the play was over, but, as the world knows, George Harrison was there for the duration. He'd been in the year below Lowe and McCartney at the Institute, but he owned an electric guitar and amplifier, and his fretboard skills had been the most advanced of any Quarry Man – "though that isn't saying very much," qualified Paul, "as we were raw beginners ourselves." Yet, even before McCartney's sponsorship had brought Harrison to the group, the idea of an Everly Brothers-type duo with George may have crossed Paul's mind – and, before teaming up with John, a McCartney–Harrison songwriting liaison had borne half-serious fruit.

Overtures from other combos for George's services had been among factors that had led to the unnoticed dissolution of The Quarry Men, but, for reasons he couldn't articulate, Harrison was to commit himself exclusively to not so much a working group as a creative entity whose principal audience was a tape-recorder in the living room at 20 Forthlin Road.

After Paul had fiddled with microphone positioning, the valves warmed up to this or that new composition, attributed to him and John, regardless of who'd actually written it. Of these works, all that remain are mostly just titles – 'That's My Woman', 'Just Fun', 'Looking Glass', 'Winston's Walk', anyone? One that survived, Paul's 'Cayenne', was, like a lot of the others, an instrumental that took up the slack of The Shadows, very much the men of the moment in early 1960. If backing group to Cliff Richard, a more comfortable British Elvis than Tommy Steele had been, they'd just scored the first of many smashes in their own right.

Perhaps when they'd acquired a more professional veneer (and a drummer) accompanying a Cliff Richard sort was the way forward for Paul, George, John – and Stuart Sutcliffe, an art student who Lennon had stampeded into hire-purchasing an electric bass guitar for what it looked like rather than its sound. Sutcliffe's arrival in their midst had followed Lennon's proposal that Harrison switch to bass. This had had as much effect as if he'd suggested an Indian sitar. John didn't even bother sounding out McCartney for whom "bass was the instrument you got lumbered with. You didn't know a famous bass player. They were just background people."

Paul would maintain that Sutcliffe "was kind of a part-time member because he'd have to do his painting, and we'd all hang out, and Stu would come in on the gigs." Though he was thus a rock 'n' roller, Sutcliffe moved too in beatnik circles, consuming specific paperback books rather than records. Though not even a pretend beatnik himself, Paul McCartney was caught in the general drift, but actually read some of the literature bought merely for display by others.

Sometimes, he got stuck as his brow furrowed over Soren Kierkegaard, the Danish mystic, and his existentialist descendants, chiefly Jean-Paul Sartre. Because it contained more dialogue, Paul was far keener on Kerouac and Burroughs, foremost prose writers of the "Beat Generation" as well as associated bards such as Corso, Ginsberg and Ferlinghetti. Now a television scriptwriter, Johnny Byrne, one of Merseyside's arch-beatniks, went further: "I fell in with a group of people who, like me, were absolutely crazy about books by the beats. We were turning out our own little magazines. In a very short time, we were into jazz, poetry – straight out of the beatniks – and all around us were the incredible beginnings of the Liverpool scene."

While this was to become homogeneously Liverpudlian in outlook, beatnik culture in general was as North American as the pop charts. Moreover, in most cases, it was intrinsically as shallow in the sense that it wasn't so much about being anarchistic, free-loving and pacifist as being seen to sound and look as if you were. With practice, you would insert "man" into every sentence, and drop buzz-words like "warmonger", "Zen", "Monk", "Stockhausen", "Greco",

"Bird", "Leadbelly" and "Brubeck" into conversations without too much affectation.

A further "sign of maturity" was an apparent "appreciation" of either traditional or modern jazz, but the nearest McCartney, Sutcliffe, Lennon, Harrison and the tape-recorder got to it was black, blind and heroin-mainlining Ray Charles who, as The Twisted Voice Of The Underdog, caused the likes of Kerouac and Ginsberg to get "gone" on 'Hallelujah I Love Her So', 'Don't Let The Sun Catch You Cryin' and the "heys" and "yeahs" he traded with his vocal trio, The Raelettes, during 1959's 'What'd I Say', with all the exhorter-congregation interplay of an evangelist tent meeting. Jerry Lee Lewis and Little Richard were products of the same equation, but they didn't punctuate their catalogues of vocal smashes with instrumental albums and collaborations with such as Count Basie and Milt Jackson of The Modern Jazz Quartet.

Through John and Stuart, midday assaults on the works of Charles and other favoured pop entertainers were heard in the life room at the art college. Another place to rehearse was the flat Stuart shared in Hillary Mansions along Gambier Terrace within the college's environs. For a while, John dwelt there as well before returning to Woolton. It went without saying, however, that he and his ensemble could still use Gambier Terrace, said Rod Jones, another tenant, "to make a hell of a lot of noise" to the exasperation of two middle-aged ladies on the ground floor.

It also reached the ears of Johnny Byrne, one of the organisers of poetry readings accompanied by local jazz musicians at Streate's. Further jazz-poetry fusions took place at the Crane Theatre. One presentation there was at the behest of Michael Horovitz who launched 1959's *New Departures*, a counterculture poetry magazine: "At the party afterwards, Adrian Henri, who was the host, said, 'Oh, this poetry stuff is all right, I think I'm going to start doing it.' Roger McGough had read with us in Edinburgh – and Brian Patten, who'd sat in the front row of the Crane gig trying to hide his school cap, was this marvellous boy who came up and read rather different, passionate, romantic poems."

While they weren't exactly "jazz", Lennon, Sutcliffe and their two pals from the Institute framed the declamations of Brighton's *vers libre* bard Royston Ellis in the Jacaranda's bottle-and-candle cellar. Afterwards, he introduced them and other interested parties in the Gambier Terrace fraternity to a particularly tacky way of getting "high" with the aid of a Vick nose-inhaler from the chemists. You isolated the part of it that contained a stimulant called benzadrine. This, you then ate.

While each tried not to put his foot in it with some inane remark that showed his age, Paul and George went along with this and other bohemian practices of the big boys from the college as they cut classes for not only rehearsals but simply to sit at one of the kidney-shaped tables in the Jacaranda, proudly familiar as John Lennon held court. The pair pitched in too when proprietor Allan Williams required the painting of murals in the basement.

Services rendered to Williams were in exchange for his acting in a quasi-managerial capacity for Lennon et al who now called themselves The Silver Beatles. The two most willing to picket for more bookings were Paul and Stuart. With silver-tongued guile, they'd lay on their "professionalism" with a hyperbolic trowel, either face-to-face or in letters when negotiating with this quizzical pub landlord or that disinterested social secretary. To this end, while they spurned the synchronised footwork with which The Shadows iced their presentations, The Silver Beatles were at one with an ancient *New Musical Express* dictum concerning "visual effect". "Some sort of uniform is a great help," it ran, "though ordinary casual clothes are perhaps the best as long as you all wear exactly the same."

On settling for black shirts, dark blue jeans and two-tone plimsolls – strictly off-the-peg chic – all they needed now was the drummer they'd lacked since they were Quarry Men. They secured one of uncertain allegiance in Tommy Moore, a forklift truck driver at Garston Bottle Works. Impossibly ancient at 26, he would suffice until the arrival of someone more compatible with young "arty" types like The Silver Beatles with their long words and weaving of names like Modigliani and Kierkegaard into conversations that would lapse into student vernacular. Not over-friendly, Moore preferred the no-nonsense society of Cass and his Cassanovas,

Gerry And The Pacemakers and other workmanlike semi-professionals who derided The Silver Beatles as "posers".

McCartney and Lennon's pretensions as composers caused comment when reputations were made much more easily by churning out rock 'n' roll standards and current hits. One of 1960's summer chart-toppers was 'Three Steps To Heaven' by Eddie Cochran, a US classic rock latecomer, whose long-awaited tour of Britain's "scream circuit" was freighted with an indigenous supporting programme made up mostly of clients on the books of Larry Parnes, one of Britain's most colourful pop managers.

On the bill too was Tony Sheridan, a 19-year-old singing guitarist from Norwich. After the final date in Bristol on 17 April 1960, Sheridan had been "stranded alone in the dressing room when everyone else had gone. For the first and last time in my life, I'd bought myself a bottle of whiskey, and was trying to vent my frustration at being an inferior British musician by getting sloshed. In the end, I smashed the bottle against the wall – but the next day, I was alive and well."

Cochran, however, wasn't, having perished when his taxi swerved into a lamp-post whilst tearing through a Wiltshire town in the small hours. "Sympathy sales" assisted the passage of 'Three Steps To Heaven' to Number One, just as they had 'It Doesn't Matter Any More' by Buddy Holly – snuffed out in an air crash – the previous year. Like Holly too, Cochran was more popular in Europe than on his own soil. In the same boat was one of Eddie's fellow passengers on that fatal journey, Gene Vincent, who paid respects with a heavy-hearted 'Over The Rainbow' when, on 3 May, he headlined a three-hour spectacular at a 6,000-capacity sports arena in Liverpool, supported by an assortment of Larry Parnes ciphers and some first-division Scouse groups procured by Allan Williams.

When the show was over, "Mister Parnes Shillings And Pence" had charged Williams with procuring an all-purpose backing outfit for use by certain of his singers for some imminent runs of one-nighters in Scotland. Among those who auditioned successfully the following week were a Silver Beatles that Allan agreed had much improved. He hadn't actually been there, but it had been reported that they'd worked up a wild response from a full house of 300 at the Casbah, a basement club in leafy Hayman's Green, run by a Mrs Mona Best, mother of the drummer in the house band, The Blackjacks.

Therefore, within three weeks of the Gene Vincent extravaganza, The Silver Beatles were north of the border for eight days in the employ of a vocalist with the stage alias "Johnny Gentle".

To use an expression peculiar to the north, Jim McCartney had "looked long bacon" when his son had announced that he was interrupting "A" level revision to go on the road with John Lennon's gang and this risible Gentle man. Like the younger Silver Beatles, Paul was even going to give himself a stage name too – "Paul Ramon", for heaven's sake. All that could be hoped was that the trip would flush this Silver Beatles nonsense out of him.

In the no-star hotels where The Silver Beatles would repair each night, Paul, like all the others, "wanted to be in a room with John". The week also coincided with Sutcliffe being temporarily *persona non grata* with the mercurial Lennon. Going with the flow, McCartney no longer had to contain a pent-up resentment of Stuart. Spiking it with the diplomacy that would always come naturally to him, Paul would "remember the first argument we really had. We came down to breakfast one morning, and we were all having cornflakes and sort of trying to wake up. Stu wanted to smoke a cigarette, and I think we made him sit at the next table: 'Oh bloody hell, Stu, come on, man! You know we're having cornflakes. Do us a favour.' There was a sort of a flare up, but, you know, we soon got back together. There was never anything crazy, and we got on fine."

Tommy Moore, however, had had more than enough of being a Silver Beatle. His resignation after the expedition put paid to the group next going to work with Dickie Pride, a diminutive Londoner whose trademark convulsions on stage had earned him the sub-title "The Sheik Of Shake".

Back on the trivial round of suburban dance halls, Paul volunteered to beat the skins before and after the loss of Moore's successor, a picture-framer named Norman Chapman, after only three weeks. Despite hardly ever sitting behind a kit before, McCartney was quite an adroit sticksman. He would also pound available yellow-keyed upright pianos, amplified by simply shoving a microphone through a rip in the backcloth.

While he was one rhythm guitarist too many as well, his and John's respective tenor and baritone were the voices heard most during any given evening. A hybrid of plummy ex-choirboy and nose-blocked Scouse, Paul was genuinely surprised when his singing caused some of the sillier girls beyond the footlights – if there were any – to make unladylike attempts to grab his attention. He wasn't impervious to their coltish charms, far from it, but was, nonetheless, aware of how brittle such adoration could be. Symptomatic of the new pestilence now ravaging the record-buying public, a TV series entitled *Trad Tavern* filled the 30 minutes once occupied by *Boy Meets Girls*.

A sure sign of stagnation in pop is adults liking the same music as teenagers. *Trad Tavern* appealed to both – and, while they might not have bought their records, grandmothers warmed to Ronnie Carroll, Mark Wynter, Craig Douglas and others from a mess of UK heart-throbs in the early 1960s who took their lightweight cue from the States. Some breached the Top Ten, but hovering between 20 and 40 was more their mark.

Amidst all the trad and Bobby candyfloss were the kind of big-voiced ballads and singers that had preceded 'Rock Around The Clock'. As much a culmination of all that had gone before as a starting point for what followed (as The Beatles would be), even Elvis succumbed in 1960 with 'It's Now Or Never', an adaptation of 'O Sole Mio', a schmaltzy Italian job from the 1900s – and his biggest hit thus far.

1960 also accommodated Top Ten debuts by Roy Orbison ('Only The Lonely'), Liverpool comedian Ken Dodd (in "serious" mode with 'Love Is Like A Violin') – and Matt Monro, whose 'Portrait Of My Love' had been made under the supervision of George Martin, recording manager of Parlophone, an EMI subsidiary, which usually traded in comedy and variety rather than outright pop. Monro, Ken Dodd and Roy Orbison were exceptions, but it was a sweeping adult generalisation that the common-or-garden pop singer "couldn't sing". That was the main reason why they loathed another hit parade newcomer, Adam Faith, the most singular of our brightest post-skiffle stars. Yet his verbal contortions and less contrived wobbly pitch had enough going for it to lend period charm to his 'What Do You Want' breakthrough and even 'Lonely Pup In A Christmas Shop' – "a ridiculous, stupid thing to do," he'd shrug in his 1996 life story, but still a Top Ten entry.

Such was the state of pop affairs when, shortly after the Johnny Gentle jaunt, The Silver Beatles hacked the adjective from their name, and wondered what to do next.

4 "What'd I Say?"

Trad bands were everywhere as were places they could play. With this stylistic stranglehold on many venues, it was small wonder that groups keeping the rock 'n' roll faith were open to offers from abroad – particularly West Germany where bastions of Teutonic trad (from Cologne's Storyville to Kiel's Star Palast) had converted to rock 'n' roll *bierkellers*, complete with the coin-operated sounds of Elvis, Gene, Cliff, Adam and the others.

Among difficulties encountered by the Fatherland's club owners was that of "live" entertainment. Patrons were often affronted by native bands who invested the expected duplications of US and British hits with complacent exactitude, a neo-military beat and an unnatural gravity born of singing in a foreign tongue.

Back in Britain, Cliff Richard, Marty Wilde, Dickie Pride and nearly everyone else who'd driven 'em wild on *Oh Boy!* had gone smooth as epitomised by wholesome film musicals from Cliff; Marty jubilant in his newly married state, and Dickie's 1960 album, *Pride Without Prejudice* – Tin Pan Alley chestnuts with Ted Heath's orchestra in accord with a lodged convention of British pop management that it was OK to make initial impact with rock 'n' roll or whatever the latest craze was, but then you had to ditch it quickly and get on with "quality" stuff so that your flop singles could be excused as "too good for the charts".

Yet if the average teenager was faced with a choice between Dickie Pride as third rate Sinatra's 'Bye Bye Blackbird' and Screaming Lord Sutch's 'Jack The Ripper' – "nauseating trash," sniffed *Melody Maker* – it'd be his Lordship every time. The most famous pop star who never had a hit, Sutch and his backing Savages were among few of their sort assured of plenty of work, with or without hits – or trad – and so were Johnny Kidd And The Pirates. The focal point of each was a blood-and-thunder stage act with the performances of Kidd and Sutch themselves as fervently loyal to classic rock as Lonnie Donegan was to skiffle.

The Beatles were more Johnny Kidd than Cliff Richard. Paul McCartney drew the short straw if ever they responded to a request for 'Voice In The Wilderness', 'Please Don't Tease' and other of Cliff's recent chartbusters, but Paul left a deeper wound with Kidd's 'Shakin' All Over' and party-pieces like 'What'd I Say' as a window-rattling, extrapolated finale in which he'd enhance his vocals with knee-drops, scissor kicks and general tumbling about during George's solos. Then about to form The Merseybeats in The Beatles' image, Tony Crane would recall, "McCartney had a guitar that he didn't play slung around his neck. They finished with 'What'd I Say', and he was madder than any time I've seen Mick Jagger. He danced all over the place. It was marvellous."

This was part of a transformation wrought by a 1960 season in Hamburg's cobbled Grosse Freiheit, a prominent red-light district just beyond the labyrinthian waterfront of the Elbe. As late as 1968, sending a group over for residencies in German night spots was, reckoned Jim Simpson, a noted West Midlands agent, "rather like training a 1,000m (1,100 yards) sprinter by making him run 5,000m (5,500 yards) courses." On the Grosse Freiheit, a haunt called the Kaiserkeller had struck first in June 1960 by enticing some unemployed London musicians across the North Sea to mount its rickety stage as "The Jets". Their number included Tony Sheridan – with whom The Beatles were to begin the commercial discography.

That lay a year in a future, which Paul, John, Stuart and George couldn't imagine during an endless search for work in and around Liverpool. Then, to cut a long story short, an offer came via Allan Williams of a residency in the Indra, a companion club to the Kaiserkeller, commencing in August 1960. A stipulation about a drummer was satisfied because, at the Casbah, The Blackjacks were about to disband, and, when asked, Pete Best was quite amenable to becoming a Beatle – even if, said McCartney, "he just wasn't the same kind of black humour that we were. He was not quite as Artsy [sic] as certainly John and Stu were."

As Paul had finished his "A" levels, his father supposed it was all right for him to go gallivanting off to Germany like other sixth formers might go back-packing in Thailand. Thus he and the rest boarded Allan Williams's overloaded mini-bus outside the Jacaranda, bound for the night ferry from Harwich to the Hook of Holland.

Hot-eyed with sleeplessness, they struggled with the first armfuls of careworn equipment into an Indra, pungent still with a flat essence of yesterday's tobacco, food and alcohol intake. With a face like a bag of screwdrivers, Bruno Koschmider, the proprietor, wasn't exactly Uncle Cuddles – but if his manner was cold, he did not seem ill-disposed towards The Beatles. It wasn't in his interest to be. An antagonised group might take it out on the customers.

The Beatles did not complain of any shortage of romantic squalor – well, squalor anyway – after Herr Koschmider had conducted them to three tiny rooms adjoining a lavatory in the Art Deco Bambi-Filmkunsttheater cinema over the road from the Indra. While there weren't enough musty camp beds or frayed old sofas to go round, this was where they could sleep. Like the foul coffee served – as they were to discover – behind the facade of the local police station, it would have sickened pigs, but another Liverpool outfit, Derry and his Seniors, seemed to be making do in two similarly poky holes at the back of the Kaiserkeller.

That evening, the border of light bulbs (not all of them working) round the stage were switched on, and a tired Beatles gave their first ever performance outside the United Kingdom. To their costumes, they'd added houndstooth check jackets, and replaced the plimsolls with winkle-pickers – all except for Pete who hadn't had time to buy the right gear. His gradual isolation from the others had started before they'd even reached Harwich.

After a slow start, one or two of the glum old men waiting in vain for the usual Grosse Freiheit fare of stripteasers, allowed themselves to be jollied along. A more transient clientele of sailors, gangsters, prostitutes and inquisitive youths laughed with them and even took a chance on the dance floor as they got used to the newcomers' endearing glottal intonations and ragged dissimilarity to the contrived splendour of television pop stars.

This was all very well, but, during wakeful periods after they'd retired, the full horror of The Beatles' filthy accommodation reared up in the encircling gloom. Daylight could not pierce it after Paul was jerked from the doze that precipitates consciousness by John breaking wind before rising to shampoo his hair in a washbasin in the movie-goers' toilets.

Their dismal living conditions did not prevent them from enjoying the fun that was to be had in the Grosse Freiheit mire. When the '60s started swinging, one of Paul McCartney's paternity suits emanated from the area where the night's love life could be sorted out during the first beer break. On initiating conversations with Paul, fancy-free and affectionate females were delighted that he wasn't one to deny himself casual sexual exploits. Though he had a steady girlfriend back home – Dorothy Rhone, a bank clerk – he was perpetually on the lookout for an unsteady one. Advisedly, shadowy thighs and lewd sniggering did not leap out of the pages of Paul's letters home during four months away that saw a transfer from the Indra to the plusher Kaiserkeller, where an abiding memory of Horst Fascher, Koschmider's indomitable chief of staff, was of Sutcliffe sketching secretively in a remote corner of the club, and McCartney and Lennon composing in the bandroom where, elucidated Paul, "the only things we write down are lyrics on the backs of envelopes to save forgetting them, but the tunes, rhythms and chords we memorise."

Creative advances did not correlate with personal relationships within The Beatles. John was still prone to antagonising his best friend just to see his hackles rise, but his inner ear ignored the stark truth that Stuart's playing hadn't progressed after all these months.

Had Paul expressed a recent willingness to take over on bass before the trip, the group wouldn't have been cluttered still with an unnecessary rhythm guitarist, no matter how contrasting McCartney and Lennon's chord shapes could be. If Stuart hadn't been around, Paul wouldn't have felt so redundant, just singing and gyrating with an unplugged guitar or impersonating Little Richard at the worn-out Kaiserkeller piano, from which aggravating Sutcliffe would snip wires to replace broken bass strings.

There was no let-up in the tension-charged ugliness, visible and invisible, back in the Bambi-Filmkunsttheater, more loathsome than ever with its improvised receptacles for junk food leavings, empty liquor bottles, overflowing cigarette ash, used rubber "johnnies" and dried vomit.

Germany changed The Beatles forever – though it almost destroyed them too when they hadn't even the decency to lie to Bruno Koschmider about spending their rest periods in a more uptown rival establishment, the Top Ten. He was furious to learn that its manager intended to lure them away with better pay and conditions as soon as their extended contract with the Kaiserkeller expired in December. Rather than racketeers and ruffians, the Top Ten attracted young "Mittelstand" adults – a couple of social rungs higher than "youths" – whose liberal-minded parents might drop them off in estate cars. Most of these would be collected just before midnight, owing to the curfew that forbade those under 18 from frequenting Grosse Freiheit clubs past their bedtimes.

The German administration was conscientious too about protecting minors from temptation – though it was too often the case that *Polizei* couldn't be bothered with the paperwork after catching young aliens like George Harrison, weeks away from his 18th birthday, flaunting the law. However, an ireful Koschmider's string-pulling ensured more intense interest, and George was sent home before November was out.

The Beatles seemed quite prepared to carry on without him, but the Top Ten was obliged to replace them with Gerry And The Pacemakers (straight from the civil service and British Rail rather than art college and grammar schools) after McCartney and Best were deported too – on Bruno's trumped-up charge of arson.

Though tarred with the same brush, Stuart and John had been free to go after signing a statement in German that satisfied the *Polizei* that he knew nothing about Exhibit A: the charred rag that constituted Herr Koschmider's accusation that The Beatles had all conspired to burn down the hated Bambi-Filmkunsttheater.

Lennon followed the others back to Liverpool, but Sutcliffe stayed on, moving in with Astrid Kirchherr, a German photographer to whom he was unofficially engaged. She was a leading light of Hamburg's "existentialists" – the "Exis" – whose look anticipated the "Gothic" style prevalent in the late 1970s. Exi haircuts were *pilzen kopf* – "mushroom head". Though commonplace in Germany, a male so greaselessly coiffured in Britain would be branded a "nancy boy", even if Adam Faith was the darling of the ladies with a similar brushed-forward cut.

The Exis fell for The Beatles partly because they were tacitly bored with the "coolness" of Dave Brubeck, Stan Getz, The Modern Jazz Quartet and other "hip" music-makers whose album covers were artlessly strewn about their various "pads".

Of individual Beatles, Pete was a strong-but-silent type in contrast to winsome Paul who, so Horst Fascher would insist, was the "sunny boy" of the group as he scuttled to and from microphones or lilted 'Besame Mucho', one of those sensuous Latin-flavoured ballads that, like 'Begin The Beguine', 'Sway' and 'Perfidia', never seem to go away. Generally, only the title was sung in Spanish when 'Besame Mucho', a frequent *wunche* (request) from the ladies – transported you for a few minutes from the shimmering sea of bobbing heads in the Kaiserkeller to warm latitudes and dreamy sighs and then the squiggle of lead guitar that kicked off 'Too Much Monkey Business' would jolt you back to reality – either that or Stuart's fluffed run-down into 'It's So Easy'.

A little of Stuart's singing went a long way too, and as an instrumentalist, he was as good as he'd ever get – and that wasn't good enough. Privately, he admitted as much to Astrid, adding that he had only came along for the laugh and because he was John's friend. Whatever was left for Stuart to enjoy about playing with The Beatles was for the wrong reasons. For devilment, he'd deliberately pluck sickeningly off-key notes. If Paul – and George too – thought he was the group's biggest liability, then he'd amuse himself being it. They could get John to sack him for all he cared, even if they'd slain a fire regulation-breaking audience on the last night at the Kaiserkeller.

5 "Over The Rainbow"

Before they'd departed from Hamburg so ignominiously, Paul had evolved into an outstanding showman, possessed of that indefinable something else – the "common touch" maybe – that enabled him, via a wink and a broad grin diffused to the general populace, to make any watching individual feel – for a split-second anyway – like the only person that mattered to him and his Beatles in the entire city.

There was, nonetheless, a crouched restlessness about Paul, and, however much he might have gainsaid it, he was looking out for any signpost that pointed in the direction of fame. He was even willing, so he'd intimated already to John, to play bass, even though it was a presence rather than a sound on the vinyl that crackled on the Forthlin Road gramophone, and its executants overshadowed by the higher octaves available to lead and rhythm guitarists.

Such a sacrifice would be to The Beatles' general good because, if Lennon might be closing his ears still, McCartney and Harrison had gauged Stuart Sutcliffe's limitations and could hear what was technically askew – and always would be. On stage at the Kaiserkeller, he'd usually been miles away mentally. More than ever before, he was physically elsewhere too – so much so that it had been necessary to line up an understudy in Colin Millander, a former Jet who had stayed on as part of a duo in a nearby restaurant. Though three years Stuart's junior – when such a difference mattered – George's exasperation that "he was in the band because John conned him into buying a bass" had shown itself in desultory sabre-rattling with Sutcliffe in safe assurance that Paul would support him when John intervened.

Paul, see, was Stuart's truer enemy. Their animosity boiled over after the latter lost his temper when McCartney, seated at the piano, made some remark about Astrid. Flinging down his bass, Sutcliffe bounded across the boards, mad fury in his eyes, to knock the detested Paul off his perch. Manfully, the others kept the song going as the pair tumbled wrestling to the floor. Used to The Beatles' excesses on the boards, the audience emitted whoops of drunken encouragement and bellowed instruction as the number finished and the irresolute fight ebbed away to a slanging match and the combatants glowering at each other from opposite ends of a huffy dressing room.

Characteristically, Paul would laugh off this proclamation of an open state of warfare as a bit of a lark in retrospect: "Occasionally, we would have our set-to's, not too many really – but the major one was a fight on stage. The great thing about it was it wasn't actually a fight because neither of us were good fighters – so it was a grope! We just grappled each other, and I remember thinking, 'Well, he's littler than me. I'll easily be able to fight him.' But, of course, the strength of ten men this guy had – and we were locked. All the gangsters were laughing at us, and me and Stu are up by the bloody piano, locked in this sort of death embrace. All the gangsters were going, 'Come on! Hit him!' to either of us, and we couldn't do anything."

As events were to demonstrate, McCartney might not have been so jocular had he managed to strike a blow to Stuart's head. Indeed, he might have ended up on a charge of murder before a German judge and jury tacitly prejudiced by his nationality and hirsute appearance. The next day, however, Paul was Mr Nice Guy again, but neither he nor Stuart would forgive or forget, and, for weeks afterwards, Paul found himself casting an odd thoughtful glance at Stuart sweating over the bass when Lennon was hogging the main microphone. Who'd have thought it – Stuart sticking up for himself without John protecting him?

Yet almost all the cards were on the table when four-fifths of The Beatles reassembled back in Liverpool – "and then the thing was, 'Well, who's going to play bass?'" asked Paul. As he'd rattled the traps in the absence of Tommy Moore, so McCartney had adapted likewise to bass whenever Colin Millander or Stuart had been indisposed at the Kaiserkeller, but for their first four post-Hamburg engagements, another ex-Blackjack, Chas Newby, was roped in.

Chas was there when The Beatles were a last minute addition to a bill at Litherland Town Hall the day after Boxing Day. A lot of groups would sell their souls for a career, however it ended, that had had a night like that in it. You couldn't refute their impact on a crowd who'd been spellbound from the 'Long Tall Sally' opening until the last major sixth of the final encore. Along the way, The Beatles had stoked up the first scattered screams that had ever reverberated for them.

The Beatles were to become a fixture at the Cavern, which, for all its previous jazz dignity, was in the process of "going pop". They made their debut in February 1961 during one of the newly established lunch-time sessions. This was to be Stuart Sutcliffe's only performance at what was destined to become as famous a Liverpool landmark as the Pier Head. Its idiosyncratic reek of disinfectant, mould and cheap perfume was still on his clothes 24 hours later – as it was on those of Colin Manley, among the audience for what must have been an off-day for The Beatles who "still had Stuart with them, and they really weren't very good."

Lennon had been pleased to see Sutcliffe, but to the others their errant bass guitarist's reappearance was like that of the proverbial bad penny now that they'd experienced Chas Newby's and then Paul's – and, on one occasion, Johnny Gustafson of The Big Three's – more agile playing. Stuart was back in Hamburg by March, but an official colour was given to this by The Beatles, who were pencilled in for a four-month Top Ten season commencing on April Fools' Day. Stuart was to be on hand in negotiations between the club, the West German Immigration Office and Herr Knoop, Hamburg's chief of police. Crucially, he had to support Mona Best's badgering and Allan Williams's assurances that The Beatles were reformed characters, especially fire-bugs Pete and Paul.

While Stuart had proved useful as a mediator, "I believe to this day that he would eventually have been thrown out," said Rod Jones, expressing a commonly held view, "as soon as there was some sort of future. I'm actually surprised that he didn't go before."

Just as it was a case of when rather than if Stuart left the group, so was not replacing him, opting instead for the simpler expedient of transferring McCartney permanently to bass. Paul's low-fretted cohesion with Pete's drumming was a subliminal element of The Beatles' intensifying local popularity as word got round, and it became customary for the Cavern to fill long before they followed the trad band or whatever else was in support, to invoke a mood of a kind of committed gaiety, often with cramped onlookers assuming the dual role of accompanying choir and augmenting the rhythm section.

While The Beatles' rowdy style was now not only acceptable but demanded at the Cavern and other recurring engagements, the going was erratic elsewhere, partly because certain parochial agents had no qualms about marrying a loud R&B outfit with, say, the ubiquitous trad band, the C&W (country-and-western) of Hank Walters and his Dusty Road Ramblers, and the monologues of comedian Ken Dodd – as took place at a Sunday matinee in a cinema in Maghull, more Lancashire than Liverpool.

The Beatles would arrive too in Birkenhead, Seaforth or – for one fabled night only – Aldershot, over the edge of the world in distant Hampshire, where the cissy *pilzen kopfs* that George, Paul and John would be sporting by the end of 1961 were sometimes a red rag to those for whom an Elvis quiff was not yet a symbol of masculinity.

On the firmer turf of the Liverpool jive-hives where they were rebooked into the foreseeable future, other groups would be copying The Beatles' stagecraft and repertoire, including 'I Saw Her Standing There', an original that had dripped mostly from the pen of McCartney.

Other than that terrible journey to Aldershot, however, campaigns for UK engagements beyond Merseyside yielded next to nothing – and Paul was keenly aware that his group's present state of marking time was prodding nerves at home, especially as he was still embroiled in hire-purchase payments for his equipment, and his income from The Beatles was far less than Mike's as a hairdresser.

Not helping either was the cost of a Hofner "violin" bass that Paul had bought from a Grosse Freiheit shop. This didn't leave much change from his earnings at the Top Ten.

Among The Beatles' duties there was backing Tony Sheridan both on stage – and in the studio after he was offered a recording contract by Bert Kaempfert, a power on Polydor, a division of Deutsche Grammophon, Germany's equivalent of EMI.

As a composer, 36-year-old Bert had contributed to 'Wooden Heart', Elvis Presley's European spin-off 45 from the movie soundtrack of *GI Blues*, a fictionalisation of his military service in Germany. The King acknowledged the melodic debt 'Wooden Heart' owed to the traditional 'Muss I Denn Zum Stadtele Naus', by breaking into German for a couple of verses.

Like nearly everybody else, The Beatles inserted a token song in German into the proceedings in Hamburg. The line of least resistance in this respect was for Paul to sing 'Wooden Heart', but more erudite was his 'Falling In Love Again' from the 1943 Marlene Dietrich movie vehicle, *The Blue Angel*. McCartney excerpts from stage and film musicals also impinged on otherwise frenetic hours on the boards. 'Summertime' (from *Porgy And Bess*) and, when that was dropped, 'Till There Was You' (*The Music Man*) and 'Over The Rainbow' could silence the most rumbustious crowd like a mass bell in Madrid.

A few Lennon–McCartney efforts were unveiled publically – two in as many hours by late 1962 – but though 'I Saw Her Standing There' became something of a fixture during The Beatles' later Hamburg seasons, it hadn't the immediacy of 'Twist And Shout', another from The Isley Brothers, or 'Shimmy Shimmy' by The Orlons, and other more ardently anticipated crowd-pleasers. Where did songwriting get you anyway? No one paid attention to an home-made song, least of all Bert Kaempfert on the prowl on behalf of Polydor for a bargain-basement "Beat Gruppa" rather than the preferred orchestra for Tony Sheridan's first single.

Bert put his head round the door at the Top Ten during one of many transcendental moments that could not be recreated, that would look impossible if transcribed on manuscript paper. By today's standards, the sound *per se* was puny yet harsh and atrociously distorted as Tony and The Beatles battled with amplifiers of 30-watts maximum that were sent through speakers known to tear, explode and even catch fire because of power surges and the mismatch of British and German ohms. McCartney would recall that "If we had troubles with our overworked amplifiers – we had to plug two guitars into the same one – I'd just chuck it all in and start leaping all round the stage or rushing over to the piano and playing a few chords."

Despite off-putting technical problems, Sheridan was to remember that "Bert Kaempfert came for several nights. He was impressed by what he thought was our authenticity – which, of course, was second-hand American music infused with elements of our own that were authentic. Afterwards, we discussed with Bert what we ought to record. I'd heard Gene Vincent do 'My Bonnie' – very differently

– and later on, a Ray Charles version. Long before we'd even thought about recording it ourselves, we'd done a sort of Jerry Lee Lewis-type arrangement on stage, but without piano. The B-side was the signature tune of my Norwich skiffle group, The Saints."

Tony Sheridan's was the name on the orange Polydor label when these rocked-up versions of 'My Bonnie Lies Over The Ocean' and 'When The Saints Go Marching In' were issued as a single in October 1961. So began Paul McCartney's recording career – helping Tony, Pete, John and George make the best of a couple of so-so numbers intended purely for Germany. It looked like being the only disc on which he'd ever be heard too.

6 "Some Other Guy"

As things turned out, 'My Bonnie' wasn't to be the only disc Paul and The Beatles would make. The Tony Sheridan single sold sufficiently to warrant an album containing some other tracks with The Beatles. There was also to be an associated extended-play (EP) disc, also entitled *My Bonnie*.

Import copies were spun by Bob Wooler, one of the disc-jockeys at the Cavern, and consolidated The Beatles' regional fame within a radius of about 25km (15 miles). Now they'd rid themselves of Stuart Sutcliffe, the group epitomised the two guitars–bass–drums archetype of what would go down in cultural history as 1963's Merseybeat explosion. They also moved up a further rung or two through their acquisition just before Christmas 1961 of a manager in 27-year-old Brian Epstein, a sales manager at his grandfather's central Liverpool department store, which contained what could be deservedly advertised as "The Finest Record Selection In The North". Until then, The Beatles had made do with Mona Best, who was efficient enough, but, as she herself realised, didn't have the entrepreneurial contacts and know-how to remove The Beatles from the Liverpool–Hamburg grindstone.

With the advent of Epstein, her say in the group's affairs was diminished to the point of eventual silence, despite vainglorious efforts for it to be otherwise, especially as her handsome Pete was, Mona believed – with much justification – the most effusive fount of the group's teen appeal. Because Mrs Best was of far less use to them now, "John, Paul and George resented her interference," said Bill Harry, editor of *Mersey Beat*. Why couldn't all Beatle women be more like Paul's uncomplaining Dorothy Rhone, who supplied occasional passive glamour when he made her sit on a bar-stool in the midst of The Beatles? Yet for all her apparent acquiescence, it had still been necessary for Paul to suspend his routine philanderings when she and John's future wife, Cynthia Powell, visited Hamburg during the months at the Top Ten.

It was John and Paul, rather than John and Stuart nowadays as, with their girlfriends, they went on picnic excursions by train on hot afternoons to seaside resorts like Ostsee where they would recharge their batteries for the labours of the night. If there was no work that evening, they'd travel further to Timmendorf Strand where it was sometimes mild enough to sleep on the beach.

Serenities like this would be few and far between after McCartney and Lennon – and Harrison – could no longer venture into a public place without the pestering of fans and reporters. In unconscious preparation, they took in their stride Brian Epstein's moulding of them into entertainers destined ideally to emerge from provincial oblivion. The Germans have a word for what Brian was doing: *verharmlosen*, to render harmless.

By March 1962, the black leathers – aggressively redolent of Nazi officer trench-coats or motor-bike hoodlums – had been superseded by tweed suits of nondescript design. These, however, were a holding operation for the following year's epauletted jackets with no lapels, that buttoned up to the throat, and had no unsightly bulges in the high-waisted trousers owing to the absence of pockets around tight hips. While the basic pattern had been taken from a blue-brushed denim get-up sold in the Hamburg branch of C&A's, that The Beatles had consented to wear it was down to the fastidious Epstein assuring them that it was for the best.

Thanks to Brian's persistence via telephone and post, the group had also risen to the challenge of the ballroom circuit, becoming a reliable draw as their booking spectrum broadened intermittently to Yorkshire, Wales and as far south as Swindon. Courtesy of Epstein's dogged prodding of Polydor's UK outlet too, 'My Bonnie' by Tony Sheridan and The Beatles was released in Britain on 5 January 1962. *NME* reviewer Keith Fordyce was generous – "both sides are worth a listen for the above-average ideas" – but, unaired on either the Light Programme or Radio Luxembourg, the disc sank without trace.

In June, the same was in store for 'You Got What I Like' by Middlesex's Cliff Bennett And The Rebel Rousers, but Parlophone seemed to regard the group as a long-term investment because it was prepared to risk another six singles before reaping the harvest of its faith in X-factor Bennett, highly regarded as a bandleader, and one of few Britons who imagined that they had a black soul within a white skin, that could actually take on black pop without losing the overriding passion.

Yet chart recognition of this seemed a far-fetched afterthought to Cliff when he and his Rebel Rousers were on the wrong side of the North Sea, putting on the agony night after night at Hamburg's new Star-Club where Paul and John of The Beatles promised to give him a leg up by writing him a song if their group got famous before his did.

Both the southern and northern English factions at the Star-Club were mixing socially with Little Richard and Gene Vincent as each disturbed Tony Sheridan's reign as incumbent rock 'n' roll king of the Grosse Freiheit. Like Caesar deified by the Gallic peasants, Richard would offend none by refusing gifts pressed upon him. One such gift was one of Paul's best shirts after "I developed a specially close relationship with Paul. He would just look at me. Like he wouldn't move his eyes – and he'd say, 'Oh, Richard, you're my idol. Let me touch you.' He wanted to learn my little holler, so we sat at the piano going 'Oooooooh! Oooooooh!' until he got it."

By the middle of the decade, Richard was to have cause to be grateful to The Beatles when they revived 'Long Tall Sally' on disc. In 1962, however, while he continued to feed off a more glorious past, they could only carry the torch of classic rock – well, their take on it – back to the confines of Liverpool.

Yet more than mere Merseybeat was unravelling there now. Following a lucrative London exhibition, abrasive Arthur Dooley had become a professional Scouser, often on BBC television's early evening magazine, *Tonight*. A protégé of Pop Art pioneer Richard Hamilton, Adrian Henri had reached beyond slapping oil on canvas to performance art and, as he had promised Michael Horovitz, poetry.

Other bards and *nouvelle vague* artists of the same vintage included Roger McGough, Brian Patten, John Gorman, Alun Owen (who was to write the script of *A Hard Day's Night*, The Beatles' first feature film), Mike Evans – and Mike McCartney who, with Gorman and McGough, had formed Scaffold, an ensemble that mingled poetry and satirical sketches during the audio-visual and literary events that, walking a tightrope between near magical inspiration and pseudo-intellectual ramblings, were springing up as alternatives to doing the 'Hippy Hippy Shake' with all o' your might down the Iron Door.

The gifted Mike was to adopt the stage surname "McGear" to stay accusations of boarding his more famous brother's bandwagon though in 1962, the two were on terms of fluctuating equality in their respective spheres. Scaffold were leading what the economist would call a "full life" with regular bookings at Streate's, the Everyman and the Blue Angel, while The Beatles were to be flown, not driven, to Hamburg for a penultimate spell at the Star-Club in November.

While the previous season had been a professional triumph, it had been blighted by the cerebral haemorrhage that had killed Stuart Sutcliffe the afternoon before their arrival. An advance party of Paul, Pete and John hadn't heard the news when they'd taken off from Liverpool. In the skies, they'd been shrill with their first BBC radio broadcast (*Teenagers' Turn* from Manchester's Playhouse) the previous weekend. Raring to go as the aeroplane descended, the three came down with a bump when Astrid Kirchherr, drained of her usual sparkle, met them after their passports had been checked. Paul was at a loss for words. Anything he said or did then wouldn't ring true somehow: "It affected John the most because he'd been closest to him. John was most disturbed by it. For me, it was a distant thing. I can't remember doing or thinking anything – but the main thing for me, that I remember feeling bad about was that he died of a brain thing. It struck me as all being Van Gogh and sort of a wild artistic thing, but I think by then, I'd got a little hardened to people dying. It wasn't like Stu was with us. We'd got used to not being with Stu – but it was a shock."

That night, Paul and Pete grizzled into their beer for a boy they hadn't understood but had liked because, outside the context of all the in-fighting, he'd come to like them.

Their eyes were still sore the next day when they went with John and Astrid to greet Brian, George and Stuart's distraught mother at the airport. A few hours later, however, The Beatles were pitching into their opening number with all their customary verve.

The next to go – albeit in less absolute terms than Stuart – was Pete Best after the group and manager had netted a hard-won recording contract with Parlophone, having been turned down by virtually every other UK company that mattered. The first session took place on 6 June in the EMI complex along Abbey Road. Like every consequent visit, it was supervised by no less than the head of Parlophone himself, George Martin, who preferred to tape pop groups in cavernous Studio Two where he'd vetoed freshening up the paintwork in case it affected the acoustics that had spiced up the chart entries of such as Eddie Calvert and Shane Fenton.

Martin's only reservations about The Beatles that first day was that he'd heard no unmistakable smash hit within their cache of Lennon–McCartney originals, and that the drummer's lack of studio experience was more pronounced than that of the guitarists. A hireling would have to ghost him when The Beatles returned to record 'Love Me Do', a McCartney opus that, for want of anything better, had been picked as the first A-side.

BBC Radio Merseyside presenter and pop historian Spencer Leigh was to devote an entire book to chronicling the saga of Pete Best's subsequent sacking. One of the lengthier chapters explores divergent theories as to why he was replaced by Ringo Starr, one of Rory Storm's Hurricanes, two months after that initial trip to Abbey Road. One of these suggests that a green-eyed monster had whispered to the other three – particularly McCartney – that Best was the fairest of them all. This was exacerbated by *Mersey Beat*'s report that, during the *Teenagers' Turn* showcase, "John, Paul and George made their entrance on stage to cheers and applause, but when Pete walked on, the fans went wild. The girls screamed! In Manchester, his popularity was assured by his looks alone."

At the stage door afterwards, Pete was almost killed with kindness by over-attentive females from the 400-strong audience while Paul, John and George were allowed to board a ticking-over charabanc after signing some autographs. Jim McCartney was on the periphery of this incident, and admonished the sweat-smeared drummer: "Why did you have to attract all the attention? Why didn't you call the other lads back? I think that was very selfish of you."

Did Mr McCartney have an indirect hand in Pete's dismissal? To what extent did his unfair reprimand – and interrelated exchanges at Forthlin Road – make dark nights of the ego darker still? He rubbed salt into the wound on observing the dismissed Best in the Cavern shadows when a Beatles bash was being documented for the ITV series, *Know The North*. "Great, isn't it!" he crowed. "They're on TV!" Pete bit his tongue and left quietly.

Jim's glee had to be contained as edited footage – of Paul, John, George and the new member doing 'Slow Down' and 'Some Other Guy' – wasn't screened until it had gained historical importance, and the concept of a Beatles without Ringo had become as unthinkable to the world as one without Pete had once been in Liverpool.

"I was a better player than him," protested Starr 30 years later. "That's how I got the job. It wasn't on no personality [sic]." Nevertheless, a session drummer had been on clock-watching stand-by for the recording of 'Love Me Do', but Ringo kept his peace just as Paul did when directed by George Martin to extend the sung hook-line, radically altering the embedded arrangement of the humble little ditty that changed everything.

7 "Till There Was You"

The release of 'Love Me Do' in October 1962 meant that The Beatles could be billed as "EMI Recording Artists", and that the glory and the stupidity of being in a 1960s pop group now necessitated being shoulder-to-shoulder in a van for hours on end during a staggered procession of one-nighters that were often truly hellish in an age when England's only motorway terminated in Birmingham.

While local engagements were becoming less frequent, the single shifted plenty in loyal Liverpool, and eventually touched the national Top 20 – just. This followed on from ITV's *Tuesday Rendezvous* on 4 December 1962, which was the first we southerners at large ever saw of The Beatles.

The follow-up, 'Please Please Me', gave more cause to hold on hoping as, before slipping in mid-March, it lingered in a Top Ten in which Frankie Vaughan, Cliff Richard, Bobby Vee and Kenny Ball were also vying to topple Frank Ifield at Number One with 'The Wayward Wind'.

Two hits in a row was sufficient to justify a long-player – which The Beatles and George Martin were expected to complete in an allotted 12-hour day with Musicians Union-regulated tea and lunch breaks during conventional London office times and an evening period with a jobsworth locking-up well before midnight.

After Gerry And The Pacemakers, The Big Three, Billy J Kramer, The Searchers, The Merseybeats and The Fourmost notched up respectable chart entries too before 1963's cool, wet summer was out, what was deemed by the media to be a "Mersey Sound" or "Liverpool Beat" gave way to a more generalised group boom, the Big Beat, also spearheaded by John, Paul, George and Ringo – EMI's "Fab Four".

The Beatles' domination of an edition of *Sunday Night At The London Palladium* drew out the agony for Decca and all the other companies who'd turned them down in 1962. Worse was to follow when the group stole *The Royal Variety Show* at the Prince of Wales Theatre on 4 November 1963 when, with McCartney's pretty 'Till There Was You' oiling the wheels, the general feeling among adults and others who hadn't wanted to like them, was that John, Paul, George and Ringo were the stock Nice Lads When You Get To Know Them.

Ireland's Bachelors – more Viscounts than Beatles – were even nicer lads who, as token pop group in the next year's *Royal Variety Show*, had been quite willing to face the Royal Box for an amended opening line – "we wouldn't change you for the wurrrrld!" – of their most recent Top Ten strike.

If The Bachelors and The Beatles put themselves in the way of potentially damaging publicity – like married Bachelor Declan Clusky's amour with a well-known female vocalist or a Liverpool woman's imputation of her baby's irregular kinship to Paul McCartney – their respective managers would ensure that no nicotine-stained fingers would type out lurid coverage of it for the following Sunday's *News Of The World*. Besides, even if it was true, nothing too sordid was likely to be yet brought to public notice about The Beatles, Gerry, Billy J, The Fourmost and other ostensibly wholesome groups by a scum press who judged any besmirching of cheeky but innocent personas as untimely: save the scandal for The Rolling Stones, who, seized by Decca, were to be a closer second to The Beatles than earlier pretenders like Gerry And The Pacemakers, The Searchers and, in early 1964, The Dave Clark Five.

As anti-Beatles, the Stones cut appositely sullen figures on the front photograph of an eponymous debut long-player – though anyone awaiting seething musical outrage was disappointed because its content didn't ring many changes. Almost as weighty with R&B standards as the first LPs by The Animals, The Yardbirds, The Kinks, The Downliners Sect, Them, The Pretty Things and The Spencer Davis Group, it even contained 'Route 66', a set-work that any self-respecting R&B aficionado now heard no more than a mariner hears the sea.

The rise of such groups – principally Londoners – was

indicative of the decline of Liverpool as a pop Eldorado by the close of 1963. Too rapid turnovers of personnel within The Merseybeats and The Big Three didn't help either at a time when teenagers needed to identify clearly with a favoured group to the extent that, ideally, the drummer toiling over his kit was as much its public face as the lead singer.

Striking while the iron was lukewarm, all manner of German labels were still rushing out as much associated product as the traffic would allow. Most of it was pressed onto cheap compilations such as 1964's *Liverpool Beat*, an album featuring both Kingsize Taylor And The Dominoes and the more versatile Bobby Patrick Big Six – from Glasgow! – who were to be taken on semi-permanently to back Tony Sheridan. Some were immortalised *au naturel* at the Star-Club, while others were often hastened to a studio as soon as the final major sixth of the shift had reverberated so that their adrenalin could be pumped onto a spool of tape.

On the rebound from a night on stage, Kingsize Taylor and his boys thought nothing of banging out an entire LP in four hours from plug-in to final mix. Certainly, they came closest here to capturing the scintillatingly slipshod power forged unknowingly from the Star-Club fracas, day after day, week upon week.

As Taylor did, Cliff Bennett could have continued making a good living in Germany, but he preferred to take his chances at home where he and The Rebel Rousers aroused the interest of Brian Epstein who, encouraged by his runaway success with the cream of Liverpudlia, was eager to diversify. With this entrepreneurial muscle behind them, Cliff's seventh single, a tougher Anglicised copy of The Drifters' 'One Way Love', tore into the Top Ten in autumn 1964, but a second bite at that particular cherry wouldn't present itself for another two years.

Thus Cliff and his group weren't to secure a slot on 1965's "*NME* Pollwinners Concert" at Wembley Empire Pool on a bill that embraced what was then the very upper crust of British pop – including The Rolling Stones, The Kinks, Twinkle, The Animals, Them, The Searchers, Georgie Fame, Tom Jones, Wayne Fontana And The Mindbenders, The Moody Blues, Donovan, Herman's Hermits, Dusty Springfield, Freddie And The Dreamers, Cilla Black – and, of course, The Beatles who closed the show.

This afternoon extravaganza on 11 April 1965 encapsulated, I suppose, the beat boom at its hysterical, electric high summer. An act drowned in tidal waves of screams that, while subsiding to mere cheers for Twinkle, Dusty and Cilla, hurled rampaging girls towards crash barriers where they'd be hurled back again by flushed bouncers, shirt-sleeved in the heat, and aggravatingly nearer to Mick, Georgie, Tom, Wayne, Ray, Donovan and Paul than those who'd give their souls to be. In the boiling mêlée further back, unluckier ticket-holders burst into tears, rocked foetally, flapped programmes and scarves, hoisted inexpertly daubed placards, tore at their hair, wet themselves and fainted with the thrill of it all.

8 "Nobody I Know"

Bing Crosby, that most influential of pre-war singers of popular song, hadn't realised that The Beatles composed their own material. Until he did, he shared the view of evangelist Billy Graham – and every other right-thinkin' North American adult – that they were just "a passing trend". Crosby was to be sufficiently impressed by The Beatles to record an idiosyncratic 'Hey Jude', but wasn't so anxious to return to the charts that he was driven to sift through their albums and, if lucky, demo tapes for a potential smash.

Among the most conspicuous chart climbers for Bing's favourite singer, Matt Monro in the mid-1960s was the first ever cover of 'Yesterday', subject of over a thousand subsequent versions. As early as March 1967, it was approaching 500 as announced by Dick James, director of Lennon and McCartney's publishing company Northern Songs.

"I just fell out of bed and it was there," divulged Paul. "I have a piano by the side of my bed, and I just got up and played the chords. I thought it can't just have come to me in a dream. It's like handing things in to the police; if no one's claimed it after six weeks, I'll have it." 'Yesterday' was then launched into life with the provisional title of 'Scrambled Eggs' until the tailoring of lyrics that McCartney sang on disc accompanied by his own acoustic guitar strumming – and a string quartet, an early example of Beatles augmentation of conventional beat group instruments. Sitars, horn sections, orchestras, tape collage and other resources were yet to come.

Matt Monro's big band rendering of 'Yesterday' made the UK Top Ten in the teeth of a belated rival 'Yesterday' on Decca by Marianne Faithfull – with an accompanying choir – that was advantaged by apparent endorsement by sole composer Paul McCartney. First refusal, however, had been given to Billy J Kramer ("it was too nicey-nicey for me") before 'Yesterday' was offered to Chris Farlowe, a white Londoner who was, nevertheless, bruited as "the greatest Blues Singer in the world today". Marianne Faithfull had dithered over it too. Then Matt Monro's headlining spot on *Sunday Night At The London Palladium* settled the matter – though McCartney's blueprint on the soundtrack album of *Help!*, The Beatles' second movie, scored in the States.

It was George Harrison's task to introduce 'Yesterday' on stage, viz, "For Paul McCartney of Liverpool, opportunity knocks!". George and the others had nicknamed Paul (not always affectionately) "The Star", partly because he seemed to have the most highly developed instinct – and desire – for gliding on the winds of showbusiness protocol whilst gilding the image of loveable and slightly naive lads from back-of-beyond taken aback by their celebrity. His skill for combining necessary ruthlessness with keeping his popularity intact was freeze-framed in an episode centred on him at the window of a chartered aircraft that had just landed somewhere in the American Midwest.

A reception committee of town burghers and their hoity-toity children are waiting on the tarmac. Behind the glass, Paul is waving and smiling. From the side of his mouth, however, he is issuing instructions to Mal Evans, a principal of the road crew, to tell the assembly outside that he – Mal – had decided that, though The Beatles were delirious with joy at the thought of meeting them, they were in need of rest for that evening's show. I'm sorry you're disappointed, but, for their own good, I've had to disappoint the boys too. Thus Evans rather than Paul, John, George or Ringo was the *bête noire* via a strategy worthy of the most battle-hardened public relations officer.

Of all The Beatles too, Paul was the one most abreast with contemporary trends such as the injection of Oriental sounds into pop as originated by either The Yardbirds – or The Kinks on 1965's 'See My Friends' with its plaintive, whining vocal and droning guitars. Their lead guitarist Dave Davies would recall an encounter in a London club, the Scotch of St James, when "McCartney said, 'You bastards! How dare you! I should have made that record.'"

Above all, however, Paul listened hard to black soul music. "Paul loves Tamla Motown," Michael Jackson would observe when he and McCartney were friends. "He also loves gut music: early, early American black music like Elmore James – but if you want to see him smile, just start talking to him about 1960s Motown. He says he was a fan like everybody else – and since those years were really important to his career, his memories are very sharp, very sensitive about that time."

On the bill of the German leg of The Beatles' final world tour in 1966, Cliff Bennett And The Rebel Rousers' set contained 'Got To Get You Into My Life', presented to Cliff in a dressing room one night by Paul McCartney on guitar and vocal, and John Lennon dah-dahing a horn section. Whereas The Beatles had attempted Motown on disc with such as Barrett Strong's 'Money', 'Please Mr Postman' from The Marvellettes and The Miracles' 'You Really Got A Hold On Me' (all on 1963's *With The Beatles*) this new offering was a Lennon–McCartney original – "one of Paul's best songs," said John – in the more ebullient of Motown house styles. Produced by McCartney, this "best song I ever recorded" was to be Cliff's biggest smash, coming within an ace of Number One in Britain.

"When John and I first started writing songs," conceded Paul, "everything was a nick. Now that's a tip for budding songwriters. We pinched ideas from records all the time. There's nothing immoral or dishonest about it because the imitation's only a way of getting started. Like, you might hear 'Please Mr Postman', and be knocked out by it, and want to do something in that style – so you could start with a line like, 'Sorry, Mr Milkman...' By the time the song's finished, you've probably got rid of the first line anyway. Maybe it doesn't sound even remotely like The Marvelettes either, but it's got you going, acted as the spark. For example, in my mind, 'Hey Jude' is a nick from The Drifters. It doesn't sound like them or anything, but I know that the verse, with these two chords repeating over and over, came when I was fooling around playing 'Save The Last Dance For Me' on guitar."

The circle remained unbroken with Beatles numbers on a Supremes album, 1965's *With Love From Us To You*, and respective revivals of 'Eleanor Rigby' and 'Lady Madonna' by Ray Charles and Fats Domino. In 1967, Charles also did 'Yesterday', which, lasting a month low in the UK Top 50, couldn't have hoped to match Matt Monro's feat two years earlier.

The rainy winter that welded 1965 to 1966 had been party time too for The Overlanders with their Paul Friswell's contention that they "did Lennon and McCartney a favour" via a faithful if unsolicited reproduction of 'Michelle', McCartney's bilingual ballad from The Beatles' *Rubber Soul* album. Friswell's cheek was mitigated when it became the first Xerox of a Beatles LP track to top the UK singles chart.

The Overlanders arrived too late for what had come to be known as the "British Invasion" of North America, which may be dated from The Beatles' landing in Kennedy airport on 8 February 1964 with 'I Want To Hold Your Hand' at Number One in the Hot 100. To the chagrin of The Beach Boys and other US acts on the same label – Capitol – John, Paul, George and Ringo had been propelled by one of the most far-reaching publicity blitzes hitherto known in the record industry. While the intruders swamped the Hot 100, The Beach Boys' resident genius, Brian Wilson had felt both threatened and inspired artistically.

"I knew immediately that everything had changed, and that if The Beach Boys were going to survive, we would really have to stay on our toes," Brian Wilson wrote in 2001. "After seeing The Beatles perform, I felt there wasn't much we could do to compete on stage. What we could try to do was make better records than them. My father had always instilled a competitive spirit in me, and I guess The Beatles aroused it."

In reciprocation, *Pet Sounds*, The Beach Boys' most critically acclaimed LP, caused The Beatles' nervous backwards glances – with Paul McCartney citing Wilson as "the real contender" rather than The Rolling Stones. Yet, during one Abbey Road session in 1966, Mal Evans was sent out to purchase *Aftermath*, the new Stones album – because, formidable though Lennon and McCartney's head start was, a year after their first original Stones A-side –

1965's 'The Last Time' – their Keith Richards and Mick Jagger had penned all 14 tracks of *Aftermath*, which would net as rich a shoal of cover singles as *Rubber Soul* had done, among them one by The Searchers, who if surviving Merseybeat's collapse, were finding it hard to crack the Top 50, let alone the Top Ten, nowadays.

If nothing else, The Searchers, Gerry, The Beatles et al had put Liverpool on the map. In doing so, the city's art scene garnered more attention than it might have done in the course of a less fantastic decade. In return, Liverpool artists remembered The Beatles at least in paintings like Sam Walsh's *Mike's Brother* (ie Paul McCartney) and *Lennon* – as well as John Edkins's *We Love The Beatles* – shown in a posthumous exhibition at the Bluecoat in 1966. Less specific homage was paid in the ritual spinning of Beatles tracks during intermissions after the Cavern was refurbished that same year to host mainly poetry readings and like soirées.

Among recurrent acts now was the mixed-media aggregation known as "The Liverpool Scene", founded by Adrian Henri and – epitomising the passing of the old order – ex-members of beat groups, The Roadrunners and The Clayton Squares. Bringing satirical humour as well as pop music to an audience that was biased against one or the other, The Liverpool Scene drank from the same pool as fellow latter-day Cavern regulars, The Scaffold who, still containing Paul's Brother, were to harry the UK Top Ten via the vexing catchiness of 'Thank U Very Much' – a response, apparently, to Paul giving Mike a Nikon camera – 'Lily The Pink' and 1974's 'Liverpool Lou'.

Over in Hamburg, there was more of a *fin de siècle* tang in the air whether Kingsize Taylor on the verge of making despondent tracks back to England or the bunkroom above the Top Ten being vacated for a reunion party after a show at the city's Ernst Merke Halle on 26 June 1966 by The Beatles. This become impractical, but a disguised McCartney and Lennon dared a nostalgic amble along the Grosse Freiheit. As the age of Aquarius dawned, British beat groups still lingered there: doughty anachronisms still giving 'em 'Some Other Guy' and 'Besame Mucho', even as The Remo Four at the Star-Club and on *Smile!*, their 1967 Germany-only LP, crossed the frontiers between R&B and jazz. Not so adaptable, fellow Scousers Ian And The Zodiacs had followed Kingsize Taylor back to England to expire quietly after turning down 'Even The Bad Times Are Good', which picked up by Essex's Tremeloes, made the Top Five.

During the global aftermath of domestic Beatlemania, John, Paul, George and Ringo had slumped too – at least as concert performers. Much of it was down to the insufficiently amplified music being drowned by screams, but the malaise was also psychological. It was a typical journeyman musician's memory, but Paul, depressed by the monotony of it all, had glowered from the window of a hotel in Minneapolis and wondered if this was all there was, just like he had in Allerton before opportunities beyond a dead-end job like his Dad's had knocked. Imprisoned luxury in Minneapolis was just like imprisoned luxury in Milan. The Coca-Cola tasted exactly the same. If it's Wednesday, it must be Genoa. Box-office receipts could be astronomical, even when shows weren't always the complete sell-outs that they had been in 1964.

Yet, how could Paul be displeased with his lot? Even before embarking on this latest public journey, he could have dug his heels in and refused to go in the knowledge that he had enough put away for him and his immediate family to never need to work again. As a recent feature in the *TV Times* had stated: "You're a lucky man, Paul McCartney" and this had been a reference not just to his swelling fortune but his proud courtship of a dashing, flame-headed actress named Jane Asher.

She was the first daughter of the quasi-dynastic marriage of eminent Harley Street doctor Sir Richard Asher – and the Honourable Margaret Eliot, a professor at the Guildhall School of Music and Drama. Among her students had been Andrew King, future manager of The Pink Floyd and a young George Martin.

Six years after he was taken on by EMI, George produced 1956's 'Nellie The Elephant', a giggly Parlophone novelty and *Children's Favourites* perennial by Mandy Miller, star of *Mandy*, an Ealing melodrama about a deaf girl, It was significant too as six-year-old Jane Asher's debut on celluloid. Her mother's connections also assisted a maiden appearance in professional theatre in the title role of *Alice In Wonderland* at the Oxford Playhouse while Jane was still completing her education at Queen's College, just round the corner from the Ashers' five-storey home in Wimpole Street.

When she first caught Paul's eye – backstage at Swinging '63, an all-styles-served-here pop spectacular at the Royal Albert Hall – 17-year-old Jane was in transition between minor child star of stage and screen, and more mature parts, having just spent her first week before the cameras in the horror movie, *The Masque Of The Red Death*. By his own account, she was more attracted initially to Mike McCartney, but before the evening was over, Paul had seen her home and asked for a date.

For the first time in ages, he'd done the running. Compared to the skirt that had solicited him since he'd been famous, nicely spoken Jane was as a chained cathedral Bible to a cheap paperback novelette. She had "class", a maturity beyond her years reflected in a wasp-waisted confidence that charmed every other male she'd known since reaching puberty. Suddenly, Paul was escorting her to the ballet, the opera, the classical theatre and other worlds of culture once outside a son of a Liverpool cotton salesman's index of possibilities.

Yet he was a hit with urbanely elegant Margaret Asher, who, affirms Andrew King, "was the one who told McCartney that he ought to go and get his clothes in Savile Row rather than Carnaby Street". She also invited him to move into the top floor at Wimpole Street for as long as it took for him to find a place of his own, now that The Beatles were in the process of uprooting from Liverpool. This, however, turned out to be as much of a social coup – and more – for Jane's brother Peter as it was for Paul.

He'd formed a duo with another singing guitarist named Gordon Waller. Known as "Peter and Gordon", they were sound enough to be signed to Columbia, another EMI label in 1964. Through knowing Paul, they were tossed 'World Without Love', a number that had been around since he was a Quarry Man. Any song with "Lennon–McCartney" as the composing credits like a licence to print money then, so after 'World Without Love' had been ousted from Number One in Britain by Roy Orbison's 'It's Over', they were back with smaller chart entries – but chart entries all the same – in two more 1964 A-sides, 'Nobody I Know' and 'I Don't Want To See You Again', specially penned by Peter's sister's boyfriend.

Two years later, Paul gave them another opus, 'Woman', on the proviso that it be attributed to the fictitious "Bernard Webb" rather than "Lennon–McCartney", just to see if it would succeed on its more intrinsic merits. His works now on the supermarket muzak bulletin as well as the hit parade, Paul had leeway for such playful financial experiments.

Peter and Gordon were, nevertheless, on the wane by 1966 when the Ashers' lodger moved out to take up residence in a large but unostentatious Regency house along Cavendish Avenue, a convenient five minute stroll from Abbey Road. That same year, Paul also purchased – on Jane's recommendation – a rural bolt-hole where fans and media would have some search to find him. A 50km (30 mile) stretch of cold, grey sea separated the northeast coast of Ireland from High Park Farm near Campbeltown, the principal settlement on Strathclyde's Mull of Kintyre, a desolate peninsula that, through McCartney, was to become known to a wider public than it might have warranted.

Meanwhile, jetting back to Britain two days after the last hurrah at San Francisco's Candlestick Park on 29 August 1966, Paul wrestled with occupational as well as personal stock-taking. Composition for The Beatles and others seemed the most potentially rewarding direction for him then, and it had been a false economy not to buy himself an expensive reel-to-reel tape-recorder, once "too big and clumsy to lug around", so that he could construct serviceable demos of the ideas – not just songs – that were now streaming from him again. Blessed with an over-developed capacity to try-try again, he grappled with his muse, drawing from virtually every musical idiom he had ever absorbed; some of them further removed from The Beatles' Hamburg core than any Star-Club bopper could have imagined.

For hours on end at Cavendish Avenue, he'd attack melody, rhyme and less specific fragments of lyrics and music from all angles, and some would become more and more cohesive with each take. This escalating engrossment in recording caused him to buy a home studio. Soon, it was theoretically feasible for every note of an entire album by Paul McCartney alone to be hand-tooled in this electronic den.

9 "I'm The Urban Spaceman"

As Peter Asher had derived benefit from his affinity, so Barry
Miles, editor of *International Times* (*IT*), did when the cash-
strapped underground journal was bailed out with cheques
from Barry's pal, Paul McCartney, who also suggested that
an interview with him in an early edition would attract
advertising from EMI and other record labels. Moreover,
when *IT* had been sped on its way with a knees-up on a
cold October night in 1966 at London's barn-like
Roundhouse auditorium, Paul (dressed as a sheik) milled
about among both proto-hippies and celebrities like
Michelangelo *Blow Up* Antonioni (the artiest mainstream
film director of the mid-1960s), Marianne Faithfull in a
cross between nun's habit and buttock-revealing mini-skirt,
and Yoko Ono, a Japanese-American "concept artist",
who'd lately left the New York wing of something called
Fluxus. Quarter-page notices of her forthcoming exhibitions
surfaced like rocks in the stream in *IT*, but, grimaced *IT*

associate John Hopkins, "Yoko Ono's happenings were boring. She was the most boring artist I'd ever met."

In its 1967 to 1968 prime, *IT* leaked to back-street newsagents in Dullsville as the provincial sixth-former's vista to what Swinging London was thinking and doing. This was disturbing enough for Frankie Vaughan – who, incidentally, had covered 'Wait' from *Rubber Soul* – to launch a campaign to curtail the spread of the hippy sub-culture. "Hippies are leeches on society", he declared at a public meeting, spurning a flower proffered by one such leech in the audience.

Fellow Scouser McCartney begged to differ: "The straights should welcome the underground because it stands for freedom. It's not strange. It's just new. It's not weird. It's just what's going around."

Sometimes, however, it was weird, unless, of course, you'd read the books, seen the films – and sampled the stimulants – necessary for understanding. Paul's *IT* interview, for example, was bloated with gaga truisms such as "It's difficult when you've learned that everything is just the act and everything is beautiful or ugly, or you like it or you don't. Things are backward or they're forward – and dogs are less intelligent than humans, and suddenly you realise that whilst all of this is right, it's all wrong as well. Dogs aren't less intelligent to dogs, and the ashtray's happy to be an ashtray, and the hang-up still occurs."

To a readership uncomprehending, disbelieving or shocked into laughter, he also made the commendably honest admission that "starvation in India doesn't worry me one bit – and it doesn't worry you, if you're honest. You just pose. You don't even know it exists. You've just seen the charity ads. You can't pretend to me that an ad reaches down into the depths of your soul and actually makes you feel more for these people than, for instance, you feel about getting a new car."

After a field visit to Bangladesh in 1968, born-again Cliff Richard, regarded by then as almost as "straight" as Frankie Vaughan, was to concur with an uncomfortable "I don't pretend I felt any heartache for the people in the Third World or anywhere else for that matter."

Via his management, Richard had been requested to articulate the Christian perspective in *The Process*, mouthpiece of the Church Of The Final Judgement, another publication that went the rounds of sixth-form common rooms. Cliff deigned not to reply, but, in issue number five, dedicated to "Fear", Paul McCartney "was not really afraid of people nor of the world ending or anything like that. It's just fear really, a fear of fear". In parenthesis, Jane Asher confided to the same questioner that she "used to be afraid of the world ending and all that five years ago," but has since "learned not to think about it".

Yet, of all underground periodicals, McCartney's first loyalty was to *IT*. With deceptive casualness, he'd entered the life of Barry Miles through Peter Asher. Jane's pop star brother had provided finance for Miles – who encouraged you to address him by his surname then – and John Dunbar, Marianne Faithfull's first husband, to open in January 1966 the Indica Gallery and Bookstore, dealing in merchandise of avant-garde and fashionably mystical bent. A few months later, *IT* was born in its basement office.

Barry's recollections of his first acquaintance with the Beatle whose biography he was to write 30 years later, is worth quoting at length: "Paul helped the bookshop out with some loot occasionally. He made us some wrapping paper, a nice pattern. He just produced a big pile of it one day.

"I knew nothing about rock 'n' roll. When I first met McCartney, I didn't even know which one [of The Beatles] he was. The first time I really had a long talk with him was after Indica had just moved to Southampton Row in March 1966. When we were there, we saw a lot of Paul. He was almost mobbed one day, walking down Duke Street. He came beating on the door and we had to let him in, and there was this great horde of people following him. He'd been out looking for some kind of thread for Jane, who wanted it for a dress she was making.

"I thought it would be very good for The Beatles to know about avant-garde music – so I persuaded Paul to come along to a lecture by Luciano Berio at the Italian Institute. We got there and sat down, and almost immediately the press came bursting in with flashlights and so on. That was the kind of thing that happened all the time."

Miles and McCartney became close friends to the degree of an insistence by the millionaire Beatle that he stand every round whenever they, John Dunbar, Peter Asher, John

Hopkins et al spent an evening in one of few watering holes these days where Paul wouldn't have to listen with heavy patience to any stranger's starstruck twaddle.

As one who'd mixed with fustian intellectuals in Liverpool and Hamburg, McCartney wasn't ignorant of many of the well-read Barry's points of reference, and could hold his own amid the beer-fuelled polemics. Yet, his understanding of what literature was worth reading and what was not became more acute through knowing Miles and the Indica crowd. "Miles was a great catalyst," he agreed. "He had the books. We [The Beatles] had a great interest, but we didn't have the books. Once he saw that we were interested, particularly me because I used to hang out with him, he showed us new things – and I'd had a great period of being avant-garde, going off to France in disguise, taking in a lot of movies, which I later showed to Antonioni: very bizarre, but it seemed exciting at the time."

Reports of further self-improvements would raise puffy smiles of condescension from those for whom "culture" was second nature (and "pop music" and its practitioners beneath contempt). Such snobs may have assumed that Paul was exhibiting an observed reverence for what he felt he ought to appreciate, but didn't quite know why. Magnifying the gap between themselves and the common herd, they would not believe that one such as him could glimpse infinity during, say, Stockhausen's *Mikrophonie I* and *II*. Yet McCartney's devouring of such new experiences went further than just shallow dropping of names. Indeed, some of it was to infiltrate The Beatles' post-Candlestick Park output.

However, that the group was off the road didn't mean that McCartney was metamorphosing into an emaciated ascetic. His recreational pursuits were both far from sedentary and not always to do with intellectual curiosity. He and the other Beatles were as prone to untoward nonsense involving drugs and girls as any other in an elite of pop conquistadores whose disconnection with life out in Dullsville was so complete that their only contact with it most of the time was through personal managers, gofers – and narcotics dealers.

McCartney had been the last Beatle to sample LSD. "Paul is a bit more stable than George and I," explained John. "It was a long time before he took it, and then there was the big announcement." If a latecomer, Paul was the loudest of all the group in the defence of LSD – "acid" – as a chemical handmaiden to creativity: "We only use one tenth of our brains. Just think what we could accomplish if we could tap that hidden part."

You only had to tune in to the music wafting from California where LSD's paranormal sensations were being translated on the boards and on record by Jefferson Airplane, Clear Light, The Grateful Dead and further front-runners of the flower-power sound of the Haight-Ashbury – "Hashbury" – district of San Francisco. Once the musical wellspring of little beyond a few jazz clubs, the city was about to become as vital a pop capital as Liverpool had been.

During its 15-month Summer of Love, the proferring of sex and marijuana "joints" became a gesture of free-spirited friendliness, while the mind-warping effects of the soon-to-be outlawed LSD possessed its "Cavern", the Fillmore West's cavorting berserkers, shrouded by flickering strobes, tinted incense fumes and further audio-visual aids that were part-and-parcel of simulated psychedelic experience.

London sometimes surpassed this with events like the inauguration of *IT* at the Roundhouse, and, another *IT* benefit, the Fourteen Hour Technicolor Dream at Alexandra Palace on 29 April 1967 where The Move, The Pink Floyd, Tomorrow, John Children, The Flies (who urinated over the front row), the omnipresent Yoko Ono, you name 'em, appeared one after the other before tranced hippies and other updated beatniks, either cross-legged or "idiot dancing".

During the merest prelude to becoming a serious chart contender, the most exotic darling of the London Underground around this time was Jimi Hendrix, a singing guitarist who'd been "discovered" walking an artistic tightrope without a safety net in New York's half-empty Cafe Wha?, and had been brought over to England to become almost the last major icon to come in from the outside of the British beat boom.

"The very first time I saw Jimi at the Bag O' Nails," recalled McCartney, "it wasn't who, but what is this? And it was Jimi. There weren't many people in the club, but at the next gig, me, Eric Clapton and Pete Townshend were standing in this very packed audience, all come to pay homage to the new god in town."

On Paul's recommendation, Hendrix was booked for a watershed performance at the International Pop Music Festival in Monterey – an overground "coming out" of what was occurring a few miles up the coast in San Francisco. It was here that the fated Jimi's showmanship as much as his innovative fretboard fireworks spurred a gallop to international stardom.

A contrasting surprise hit at Monterey was Ravi Shankar, the Indian sitar virtuoso, whose *West Meets East* album with the equally acclaimed violinist Yehudi Menuhin was issued just before 'Norwegian Wood' and 'Paint It Black' brought the sitar to a pop audience – though Shankar had been accused already by longtime devotees of "selling out" and of emasculating his art with Grammy-winning collaborations such as this.

Just as George Harrison had been the principal advocate of the application of Indian musical theories and instrumentation (and spiritual beliefs) to The Beatles' oeuvre, so McCartney was chiefly responsible for at least superficial use of their pioneering tonalities of Berio, Stockhausen et al as evidenced in 'Tomorrow Never Knows' in which only a repeated tom-tom rataplan and Lennon's battered lead vocal endowment on its trace of melody put it into the realms of pop at all.

On the same album, 1966's *Revolver*, McCartney shone brightest on 'Eleanor Rigby' – "Paul's baby, and I helped with the education of the child," quipped Lennon. She was, however, destined to die alone – with, seemingly, no one to welcome her through the pearly gates. That was how Eleanor had always lived until she expired in the church that was her only comfort, and was buried "along with her name" with just Father McKenzie, another lonely person, who darns his own socks, in attendance. Old maids would make further appearances in the corporate and solo canon of The Beatles – almost all through the offices of McCartney, who penned the bulk of 'Lady Madonna' and all of 1971's 'Another Day'.

'Eleanor Rigby' nestled comfortably among easy-listening standards like Stevie Wonder's 'I Was Made To Love Her', Jose Feliciano-via-The Doors's 'Light My Fire', 'Brown-Eyed Girl' by former Them vocalist Van Morrison, Fifth Dimension's 'Up Up And Away', gently reproachful 'Pleasant Valley Sunday' by The Monkees, and flower-power anthems like 'San Francisco' from Scott McKenzie.

'When I'm Sixty-Four', a recreation of a Jim Mac Jazz Band-type refrain, was the item that most fitted this brief on *Sgt Pepper's Lonely Hearts Club Band*. The most celebrated of all Beatles' long-players had sprung from late Abbey Road hours of cross-fades, stereo panning, intricately wrought funny noises and similarly fiddly console minutiae when the team were at the forefront of a trend for "concept albums" (which included "rock operas" and like *magnum opi*) – though others weren't far behind.

Mere weeks after *Sgt Pepper* reached the shops, 'Grocer Jack', a kiddie-chorused excerpt from *A Teenage Opera*, composed by Mark Wirtz, once a would-be German Elvis, was in the UK singles list. Nevertheless, while this built up anticipation for an associated album and stage show, the 'Sam' follow-up barely rippled the Top 40, and another 45rpm clip didn't even "bubble under". As a result, investors lost heart and the opera was abandoned.

Joe Average has heard even less of a concept LP that was realised by Paul McCartney late in 1965. As reported in the *Disc And Music Echo* gossip column, a few copies were pressed as Christmas presents for just the other Beatles and Jane Asher. It was said to be an in-joking send-up of a radio variety show with the irrepressible Paul as a one-man compère, singer, instrumentalist, comedian and all-purpose entertainer. If it ever existed, the roots of *Sgt Pepper* may lie in this *ultima Thule*, this unobtainable prize for collectors of Beatles artefacts.

If one ever turned up in a memorabilia auction, it might bolster McCartney's assertion that it was he who came up with the basic notion of *Sgt Pepper* on a return flight from a holiday in Kenya in November 1966 – though he was to aver that "only later in the recording did Neil Aspinall [The Beatles' personal assistant] have the idea of repeating the 'Sgt Pepper' song, and The Beatles and George Martin begin to use linking tracks and segues to pull it together."

The *Sgt Pepper* era remains the principal source of countless hours of enjoyable time-wasting for those who collate "hidden messages" in the grooves and packagings of Beatles discs. While this is a subject worthy of 1,000 university theses, we can only scratch the surface here by attending to the most enduring so-called communiqué which supported a rumour that Paul McCartney had been beheaded in a road accident on 9 November 1966 and replaced by a doppleganger. All that actually happened was that he cut his lip that day in a mishap whilst riding a moped, but surely you can hear John say "I buried Paul" in a daft voice in the last seconds of 'Strawberry Fields Forever' – and at the end of 'I'm So Tired' on 1968's 'White Album' (*The Beatles*), doesn't he mumble "Paul is dead. Bless him, bless him, bless him..."?

None of them were hits, but there was soon an impressive array of "Paul Is Dead" singles behind counters. Penetrating the crowded airwaves then were the likes of 'Brother Paul' by Billy Shears And The All-Americans, 'Saint Paul' from Terry Knight – future manager of Grand Funk Railroad – and Zacharias and his Tree People's 'We're All Paul Bearers (Parts One And Two)'. In a vocational slow moment after 'Light My Fire', Jose Feliciano issued a 'Paul' 45 too. As an ex-Beatle, Lennon's snigger was almost audible when, not content with airing grievances against McCartney in the press, he sniped at him on disc in 1971 with 'How Do You Sleep' from *Imagine*, confirming that Billy, Terry, Zacharias et al were "right when they said that you were dead".

A real death, however, *had* occurred within The Beatles "family" in 1967. In need of careers advice, Denny Laine, former mainstay of The Moody Blues, arrived on the off-chance at Brian Epstein's Belgravia doorstep during 1967's August Bank Holiday. He received no answer to his knock. Inside, Brian was expiring in a drug-induced slumber.

He was found on the Sunday afternoon. At around 4pm, eight-year-old Ruth McCartney, daughter of Jim McCartney's second wife, Angela Williams, had been visiting her stepbrother and his Beatles in Bangor, a university town where the Welsh mainland nears the island of Anglesey. She and Angela had been bidding him farewell when he'd been requested to take an urgent telephone call. She was to learn its content on arrival back home in Hoylake, over the river from Liverpool, two hours later. The telephone there was ringing too. George Harrison's mum was on the line with an example of how the story had become confused. Brian, she told Angela, had shot himself.

By then, the truth The Beatles had refused to avow had inflicted itself. They could no longer not believe it. An attempt to sooth their anguish had been made by the Maharishi Mahesh Yogi, the Indian guru who'd been running the weekend course in transcendental meditation that they'd all been attending at the University of Bangor.

The appeal of a community more enclosed than the innermost pop clique was attractive enough for The Beatles to study meditation further at the Maharishi's yoga-ashram – theological college – in the Himalayas the following spring. Even prior to his association with Indica, Paul McCartney had explored Buddhism and Hinduism as well as mystical and esoteric Christianity, but had not been completely convinced by any of them. Furthermore, while he continued to practice meditation, even designating a room in his house for that specific purpose, his jet-lagged return from India was a fortnight ahead of George and John, and his most piquant memory of the visit one of a solitary session on a flat roof when "I was like a feather over a hot-air pipe. I was just suspended by this hot air, which had something to do with the meditation – and it was a very blissful thing."

Back to the day-to-day mundanities of being a Beatle, Paul was still living down *Magical Mystery Tour*, the made-for-television movie – and their first major post-Epstein project – of which he'd been both the instigator and main producer. To disaffected observers – and, indeed, to John, George and Ringo now and then, his methodology had appeared slap-dash – as if he was making it up as he went along, which he was much of the time. Concordant with the bare bones of the "plot" – summarised by the title – there was much spontaneity, improvisation and scenes that seemed a good idea at the time. Worse, though some clutter fluttered onto the cutting-room floor, direction and outcome still remained vague – but maybe that was almost the point.

The finale was a big-production number, 'Your Mother Should Know', written by Paul, and recorded the week before Brian Epstein's sudden passing. Like 'When I'm Sixty-Four', it was at one with a fad for olde tyme whimsy that had prevailed in the hit parade since 1966's chart-topping 'Winchester Cathedral' – all vicarage fête brass and posh megaphoned vocals – by The New Vaudeville Band. In its wake came such as Whistling Jack Smith's 'I Was Kaiser Bill's Batman', boutiques like 'I Was Lord Kitchener's Valet' and experiments – by The Beatles too – with dundreary side-whiskers, raffish moustaches and similar depilatory caprices that prompted a Mancunian costumier to manufacture fake ones so those without the wherewithal to sprout their own could still "Make The Scene With These Fantastic New Raves".

On the strength of their debut 45, 'My Brother Makes The Noises For The Talkies', The Bonzo Dog Doo-Dah Band ran in the same pack, but, as it turned out, they defied entirely adequate categorisation – except that, though the outfit's *raison d'être* was centred on getting laughs, they were more Scaffold than Freddie And The Dreamers in that they conveyed in pop terms that strain of fringe-derived comedy that was to culminate with Monty Python's Flying Circus.

"In 1966, we decided to expand our style," explained Neil Innes, who was, with Vivian Stanshall, the group's principal composer. "We did 1950s rock 'n' roll, flower-power, anything went – and started writing our own stuff. It only took a year to develop. If it got a laugh, it stayed in the act. On the cabaret circuit and then the colleges, and we were earning as much as any group with a record in the charts. We were liked by people like Eric Clapton as a band most of them would liked to have been in – even though we were never mega recording artists."

Their eventual modicum of Top Ten success – with an Innes opus, 'I'm The Urban Spaceman' – was testament to courage in remaining true to their strange star, but it was, however, secondary to an eye-stretching stage act, which earned them both a cameo in *Magical Mystery Tour*, and a weekly turn on the anarchic ITV children's series, *Do Not Adjust Your Set*.

"I wrote 'Urban Spaceman' in one afternoon," said Innes with quiet pride. "Our producer, Gerry Bron, was fairly strict about studio time, and Viv Stanshall complained about this to Paul McCartney, who he'd met down the Speakeasy. Paul came along to the 'Urban Spaceman' session, and his presence obliged Gerry to give us more time. Paul also had great recording ideas – like double-tracking the drums, and putting a microphone in each corner of the playing area to catch Viv's garden hose with trumpet mouthpiece as he whirled it round his head.

"I was quite keen to do a follow-up that was sort of humorous but still catchy. We selected 'Mr Apollo', which was once like that. Most of it was mine, but Viv got hold of it, and it ended up well over acceptable single length – because it wasn't until 'Hey Jude' that you could get away with it."

10 "Those Were The Days"

In Brian Epstein's final months, the same questions had come up over and over again. Plain fact was that the contract was up for renewal anyway, and, according to hearsay, his stake in Beatles affairs would have been reduced, though they wouldn't have carried on totally without him.

Therefore, though Brian might not have approved of Apple Corps, had he lived, he probably wouldn't have been able to do much to prevent it. On paper, nevertheless, it made sound sense, combining a potential means of nipping a huge tax demand in the bud and a diverting enterprise that could equal profit as well as fun. It was intended to house all manner of artistic, scientific and merchandising ventures under The Beatles' self-managed aegis. By 1970, however, this had been whittled down to Apple Records, a label whose releases were monitored by EMI.

Yet, once upon a time, Apple had been visualised as the most public expression of the underground's "alternative economy", and as much its embodiment as the free open-air rock concerts that pocked post-flower power Britain's recreational calendar. Motives, as always, were suspect. Apple, nevertheless, seemed at first to be genuinely if romantically anxious to give a leg up to those with deserving causes.

The Beatles were on such a person's side. They alone understood the difficulties of gaining recognition and finance, having had to struggle for so long themselves before George Martin lent an ear to their efforts. In addition, with Barry Miles the Aaron to his Moses in *IT*, "Paul McCartney asked me to point out that Apple exists to help, collaborate with and extend all existing organisations as well as start new ones. It is not in competition with any of the underground organisations. The concept, as outlined by Paul, is to establish an underground company above ground as big as Shell, BP or ICI, but, as there is no profit motive, The Beatles' profits go first to the combined staff and then are given away to the needy."

Apple's chief non-Beatle triumph was Mary Hopkin, whose records were produced – and, in the case of 1969's 'Goodbye', composed – by McCartney. An 18-year-old soprano, Hopkin was known already in the parallel dimension that is the Welsh pop scene. Until a winning appearance on ITV's *Opportunity Knocks*, her abilities had been directed at the Welsh-speaking market mostly via slots on BBC Wales's weekly pop showcase, *Disc A Dawn*. She began making headway east of Offa's Dyke after fashion model Twiggy brought her to McCartney's attention.

At her father's insistence, some of her B-sides were in Welsh, but her debut Apple A-side, 'Those Were The Days', was in pop's international tongue, and thus began Hopkin's three-year chart run in fine style by spending most of 1968's autumn at Number One after ending the two-week reign of seven-minute 'Hey Jude'.

John Lennon had been put in charge of another female vocalist in which Apple had been "interested". Unlike John Hopkins, he hadn't found Yoko Ono boring at all. As well as taking the place of Cynthia in his bed, Yoko also superseded Paul as a lovestruck John's artistic confrère. Through her catalytic influence, the world and his wife were confronted with a John Lennon they'd never known before, one for whom The Beatles would soon no longer count any more.

Apart from Cynthia, how could anyone begrudge Yoko and John their joy? Many did after *The News Of The World* front-paged the rear cover of *Unfinished Music No 1: Two Virgins*, the couple's first album together. It was a back view of themselves hand-in-hand – and stark naked. The front photograph was too indecent for a self-called family newspaper.

This, like the rest of John and Yoko's many funny-peculiar pranks in the name of art, didn't "give me any pleasure" wrote Paul later, but he showed cursory solidarity by accompanying John and his inseparable Yoko to an appointment with EMI chairman Sir Joseph Lockwood to discuss the distribution of *Two Virgins*. He also allowed the inclusion of a shot that almost-but-not-quite revealed all of himself too in the pull-out poster that was part of the packaging of the Beatles' 'White Album'.

It had been snapped by Paul's new girlfriend from New York, Linda Eastman. Ultimately, he'd been unlucky with Jane Asher – to whom he'd been engaged since January 1968. She'd made an unexpected entry into the Cavendish Avenue master bedroom where another young lady – a New Yorker too – clutched a hasty counterpane to herself. Paul had always been incorrigibly unfaithful; it was one of the perks of his job, but this was the first time he'd been uncovered. Nevertheless, he and Jane weren't over immediately. Indeed, they'd seemingly patched things up when they attended Mike McCartney's wedding in July, but the damage had been done, and was permanent.

A free agent again, Paul chased a few women until they caught him – albeit only fleetingly, but there was no one for the press to take seriously for several months – though it would have been quite a scoop had a tabloid editor got wind of an incident at the Bag O' Nails when McCartney attempted to chat up Rolling Stone Bill Wyman's Swedish sweetheart, Astrid.

It was in the same London night club that Linda Eastman had introduced herself to Paul in 1967 on shivering with pleasure at the smile he flashed from the other side of the room. He in turn was to be impressed by a disarming self-sufficiency that would not permit him to be bothered by the fact that she was a divorcée – and the mother of a six-year-old, Heather. In any case, it would have been hypocritical of him not to have been morally generous.

From a family of prominent showbusiness attorneys, Linda was quite accustomed to the company of professional entertainers. This was compounded by her skills as a freelance photographer, and her social intercourse with pop musicians visiting or resident in New York. She was on particularly good terms with The Animals – and the group's former bass player, Chas Chandler had been Linda's escort at the Bag O' Nails on the occasion she met Paul. Two years later, she was gripping the Beatle arm with a bright, proprietorial grin, and there was less anger than amusement from Heather's father, a geophysicist named Melvin See, when his daughter and ex-wife moved into Cavendish Avenue less than six months after the split with Jane Asher.

Beatles traditionalists did not regard this upheaval as profound an erosion of Fab Four magic as John's estrangement from Cynthia, and the entrenchment of that dreadful Yoko – with whom he was now recording chartbusting singles with an ad-hoc Beatles splinter group, The Plastic Ono Band. Her baleful presence at Abbey Road had exuded too from the needle-time on the White Album, most notably in 'Revolution 9', dismissed by most as interminable musical scribble.

As fans may have expected, Paul had been responsible for the track that mirrored *Rubber Soul*'s 'Michelle' as the biggest selling cover from the White Album, namely 'Ob-la-di Ob-la-da', inspired, so one story goes, by the Jamaican patois of Georgie Fame's percussionist, Speedy Acquaye. In March 1969, a Benny Hill television sketch centred on a disc jockey obliged to host an early morning radio show after a night on the tiles. Exacerbating his hungover queasiness was a listener's request for "any platter by Grapefruit, Cream – or Marmalade!" This gag was an illustration of the latter outfit's chart-topping success with a shrewd Yuletide copy of 'Ob-la-di Ob-la-da'. As four of this quintet were Glaswegian, they celebrated by miming it on *Top Of The Pops* in national costume: the Clydeside boys resplendent in sporrans, gorgets, clan tartans et al with their English drummer in redcoat gear as a reminder of Culloden.

Each new edition of the weekly show hammered home to Denny Laine the extent to which his fortunes had declined since he left The Moody Blues. Two solo singles had missed the charts, and Balls, a so-called "supergroup" of which he'd been a member, had bitten the dust too: "then Ginger Baker [former drummer with Blind Faith] came to my house one night and asked me to join Airforce. It was a shambles – too many players all trying to outdo one another, not enough discipline."

Baker's post-Blind Faith big band made its stage debut at Birmingham Town Hall. Most personnel stuck it out for just one more engagement – at the Royal Albert Hall – where a rambling and unrepentantly loud set was captured on tape. From this was salvaged a single, Bob Dylan's 'Man Of Constant Sorrow', sung by Laine.

Airforce was one example, but about twice a month from around the middle of 1966, the music press would report a schism in – or complete disbandment of – one group or other; either that or a key member setting himself apart from those with whom he'd been in earshot for every working day since God knows when. Manfred Mann took formal leave of Paul Jones at the Marquee; Yardbirds vocalist Keith Relf edged into the Top 50 with a solo 45, and the firing of Jeff Beck from the group wasn't far away. Another lead guitarist, Dave Davies, enjoyed two 1967 hits without his fellow Kinks, and Wayne Fontana had cast aside his backing Mindbenders. The Walker Brothers were to part after a final tour, while Brian Poole and The Tremeloes were recording separately. Alan Price had had several Top 20 entries as an ex-Animal, while Van Morrison had made a less sweeping exit from Them.

All four Beatles were uncomfortably aware that some sort of crunch was coming for them too. John's activities with Yoko and The Plastic Ono Band were bringing it closer by the day. Who could blame Paul, George and Ringo for pondering whether a relaunch as either a solo attraction or in a new group was tenable? Was it so unreasonable for Paul especially to hold in his heart that either way, The Beatles would be recalled as just the outfit in which he'd cut his teeth before going on to bigger and better things?

11 "Wedding Bells"

Weeping female fans mobbed London's Marylebone Registry Office on that dark day – 12 March 1969 – when Paul and his bride tied the knot. Next, the marriage was blessed at a Church local to Cavendish Avenue. To limit the chances of an outbreak of Beatlemania, neither George, Ringo nor John – who was to get hitched to Yoko a week later – showed up at either building, and a police raid on Harrison's Surrey home and the subsequent discovery of controlled drugs upset his plans to attend the Ritz Hotel reception.

On the BBC's *Six O'Clock News*, girls who'd witnessed the newly-weds exit from the registry office were not undismayed by the last bachelor Beatle's choice, even if most had expected it to be Jane Asher. Though their views weren't broadcast, some speculated whether or not Linda was pregnant.

She gave birth to Mary on 28 August 1969 in London, though, as it would be with half-sister Heather and two younger siblings, Mary was to look upon East Gate Farm near Rye, Sussex, as home after what would amount to eventual years of house-hunting by Paul and Linda. Cavendish Avenue, however, was to remain McCartney's principal address for at least as long as The Beatles endured – though they weren't much of a group anymore by the second half of 1969. Increasingly rare moments of congeniality occurred most frequently when not all of them were present at Abbey Road. The old brusque tenderness between Paul and John, for instance, was caught in a photograph taken during a session when, with the former on bass, piano and drums, they were the only Beatles heard on 'The Ballad Of John And Yoko'. It had been composed by Lennon as he continued painting himself into a corner with Yoko, going so far as to change his middle name by deed poll from "Winston" to "Ono" in a ceremony on the flat roof of Apple's central London office.

This was also the location of that famous traffic-stopping afternoon performance – The Beatles' last ever – with organist Billy Preston, an old pal from the Star-Club. "That idea came from the bottom of a glass," said Paul of this most captivating sequence from *Let It Be*, the *cinéma vérité* follow-up to *Help!*. Elsewhere, you could slice the atmosphere with a spade now that Paul's boisterous control of the quartet's artistic destiny had gathered barely tolerable momentum since John's unofficial abdication as de facto leader of the four.

It wasn't all smiles at business meetings either. The crux of all disagreements was that McCartney advocated his own father-in-law, Lee Eastman, to disentangle Apple and The Beatles' disordered threads, while Lennon, Harrison and Starr favoured Allen Klein, a New York accountant who Eastman – and, by implication, Paul – disliked and distrusted.

It was scarcely surprising, therefore, that each Beatle was readying himself for the end in his own fashion. Because everyone involved understood that there weren't to be any more Beatles after *Abbey Road*, a spirit of almost *Sgt Pepper*-ish co-operation pervaded. As healthy too in their way were the flare-ups that replaced the irresolute nods of *The Beatles* and *Let It Be*. Of all of them, none was so bitter as the one over Paul's 'Maxwell's Silver Hammer'. This was overruled as a spin-off single in favour of a double A-side of George's 'Something' – and 'Come Together' by John, the most vehement opponent of 'Maxwell's Silver Hammer'. It was, he thought, a glaring example of what he and George derided as "granny music".

Regardless of content, *Abbey Road* as a whole had a clearer sound than *Let It Be*'s associated album, which had been doctored by US producer Phil Spector, whose muddy bombast and heavy handed orchestration was frowned upon by McCartney, whose poor opinion was echoed by studio engineer Glyn Johns. Yet, issued out of sequence, ie after *Abbey Road*, *Let It Be* earned another gold disc for The Beatles, albeit a Beatles who couldn't care less.

12 "Love Is Strange"

"I suppose it ceased to be a working partnership months ago," admitted Paul to journalist Anne Nightingale in 1970, "but the Beatles' partnership goes on for seven more years, and this is why I want out now. The other three of them could sit down now and write me out of the group. I would be quite happy. I could pick up my cash and get out. I don't know how much is involved, but I don't want Allen Klein as my manager."

Neither for now did McCartney wish to endure the unpleasantnesses that occur when human beings congregate in a recording studio. During the mild winter that had seen in the new decade, how much more gratifying it had been to tape by multiple overdub enough for an eponymous solo album on four-track equipment in the privacy of Cavendish Avenue and his home-from-home in the Mull of Kintyre. Other than some backing vocals by Linda, Paul had sung and played every note. With the help of a manual, he had now become sufficiently schooled in the equipment's aural possibilities to commence a day's work with nothing prepared. Without the emotional overheads of working with John, George and Ringo, he layered instrument upon instrument, sound upon sound, for hours on end, anchored by a metronome or retractable "click-track".

Following some fine-tuning in "technically good" Abbey Road and a "cosy" complex in Willesden, *McCartney* was finished to the last detail – or at least the last detail its creator had any desire to etch. "Light and loose" was how he described it in a press release – a "self-interview" – that also got off his chest a lot of feelings about Lennon, Klein ("I am not in contact with him, and he does not represent me in any way") and other issues including the "personal differences, business differences, musical differences" with The Beatles.

Some of its consumers were to find a copy within a package that, after much angered to-ing and fro-ing between Paul and the Klein conclave, reached the shops in April 1970, a fortnight before the valedictory *Let It Be*, and just after *Sentimental Journey*. Without spawning a spin-off 45, *McCartney* shifted an immediate two million in North America alone, and the general verdict at the time was that it was OK but nothing brilliant. Perhaps it wasn't supposed to be, even if The Faces, fronted by Rod Stewart, thought highly enough of 'Maybe I'm Amazed' to revive it a year later (as would McCartney himself in 1976).

Overall, the album captures a sketchy freshness, even a stark beauty at times. Certainly, it was much at odds with more intense offerings of the day, whether Led Zeppelin, Deep Purple, Man, Black Sabbath, Humble Pie and other headbangingly "heavy" outfits or the "pomp-rock" of ELP, Yes and borderline cases like Pink Floyd and The Moody Blues, castigated for preferring technique to instinct – and *McCartney* couldn't be accused of that.

While the likes of Man and ELP appealed to laddish consumers lately grown to man's estate, self-doubting bedsit diarists sailed the primarily acoustic waters of the early 1970s denomination of singer-songwriters ruled by James Taylor as surely as Acker Bilk had ruled British trad jazz. While there were elements of the same self-fixated preciousness of Taylor, Melanie, Neil Young and their sort, *McCartney* wasn't anywhere as mannered in its embrace of, say, a paean to its maker's wife ('The Lovely Linda') – and *Let It Be* leftovers ('Teddy Boy') and, the first track ever aired in Britain (on *Pick Of The Pops* one Sunday afternoon), 'That Would Be Something', still being performed by McCartney in the 1990s.

Most of his first true solo effort had resulted from a kind of purposeful mucking about that didn't suggest that Paul McCartney was ready to soundtrack the 1970s as he had the Swinging Sixties with John Lennon, especially after the two's artistic separation was to be confirmed when The Beatles dissolved formally in the Chancery Division of the London High Court on 12 March 1971.

Inevitably, too much would be expected of Paul, John, George and, if you like, Ringo – but whether the much-

anticipated *McCartney, John Lennon: Plastic Ono Band*
and Harrison's *All Things Must Pass* had been tremendous,
lousy or, worse, ordinary wasn't the issue for the sort of
fan for whom just the opportunity to study each one's sleeve
was worth the whole price of what amounted to a new
ersatz-Beatle album. It was adequate that it just existed.
Nevertheless, like The Rolling Stones, Bob Dylan and Frank
Zappa, though McCartney, Lennon and Harrison would
rack up heftier sales and honours as individuals, the
repercussions of the records they'd made during the 1960s
would resound louder. Having gouged so deep a cultural
wound collectively, whatever any of them got up to in the
years left to him was barely relevant by comparison, no
matter how hard he tried.

Paul, in particular, acquitted himself well as a chart
contender, made nice music, but none of it made the
difference that The Beatles had. His first post-Beatles single,
'Another Day' – as melancholy as 'Eleanor Rigby' – zoomed
to a domestic Number Four on 4 March 1971, and began
a journey to one position short of this in the US Hot 100 a
week later. All that stood in his way to the very top in Britain
before the month was out was 'Hot Love' from T Rex, glam-
rock giants, whose "T Rexstasy" was as rampant among
schoolgirls as Beatlemania once was, and "Rollermania"
was to be when Edinburgh's Bay City Rollers – in their
gimmick bow-ties and half-mast tartan trousers – were hyped
as "the new Beatles". *Plus ça change.*

Lennon's extreme strategies had taken him beyond the pale as an orthodox pop star, while Harrison insisted that he "wouldn't really care if nobody ever heard of me again" after his finest hour at the forefront of the "Concerts for Bangla Desh" in August 1971. McCartney, however, wasn't so happy about someone else having a turn as the teenagers' – or any other record buyers' – fave rave. At the same age – 28 – Roy Orbison had been revered as something of a Grand Old Man of pop during the 1963 tour, but he'd had a receding chin, jug-handle ears and pouchy jowls like a ruminating hamster.

The allure of Paul's yet unwrinkled good looks, his hair remaining on his head, and his relative boyishness were belied only by the sorry-girls-he's-married tag that had so irritated the adulterous John before the coming of the second Mrs Lennon when "I really knew love for the first time".

Paul was happily married too, and, like John, intended his missus to get in on the act. Linda had endured piano lessons as a child, but had come to loathe the carping discipline of her teacher. Yet she was sufficiently self-contained to disassociate the music from the drudgery. Indeed, when the dark cloud of the lessons dissolved, she and her school friends had often harmonised *a cappella* for their own amusement in imitation of 1950s vocal group hits such as 'Earth Angel' (The Penguins), 'Chimes' (The Pelicans) and 'I Only Have Eyes For You' (The Flamingos).

Many other outfits of this vintage gave themselves ornithological appellations too – The Crows, The Orioles,

The Feathers, The Robins and so forth. The story goes that, with this in mind, Linda, heavily pregnant with a third daughter, modified Paul's original suggestion of "Wings Of Angels" to just plain "Wings" as a name for the group he planned to form for both stage and studio. That there was already a US entity called Wings with a recording contract too, was of no apparent consequence.

After recovering from the premature birth of Stella – named after both her maternal great-grandmothers – in London on 13 September 1971, Linda began her diffident tenure in Wings, vamping keyboards as well as ministering to overall effect as a singer. Unlike Yoko Lennon, she was a timid songbird, and wasn't willing initially to walk a taut artistic tightrope with her vulnerability as an instrumentalist. "I really tried to persuade Paul that I didn't want to do it," she protested. "If he hadn't said anything, I wouldn't have done it."

The other more experienced members recruited shared her doubts: "Linda was all right at picking things up, but she didn't have the ability to play freely. If we'd had her and another keyboard player as well, we would have been fine, but Linda was given too much to do. She was a professional though. She got paid like the rest of us."

Thus spake Denny Laine, who had been engaged on an album of his own when summoned to the Mull of Kintyre in August 1971. McCartney had first met his future lieutenant when the pre-Moody Blues Denny Laine And The Diplomats had supported The Beatles at a poorly attended booking at Old Hill Plaza near Dudley back on 11 January 1962. Each had since stayed in the picture about the other's activities, and so it was that "Paul knew I could sing, write and play, and so he called me. It knocked me sideways a little because I wasn't used to being a sidekick, but I admired Paul. That was the first time I'd been with a band with someone more famous than me."

It was also the first time Laine had been in a band with someone of the same Christian name. At the drum stool for several months before Laine's coming was Denny Seiwell, who McCartney had discovered in New York during a thin time in which the versatile Seiwell had proved equally at ease attending to "godfather of soul" James Brown's anguished raps as the easy-listening country-rock of John Denver. By 1970, however, he was living a hand-to-mouth existence in the Big Apple where the McCartneys, purportedly, stumbled upon him cluttering a sidewalk along the Bronx. "We thought we'd better not pass him by," recalled Paul-as-Good Samaritan, "so we picked him up, put him on a drum kit, and he was all right."

There was another more pragmatic reason for taking him on. "The other New York session guys Paul had approached wanted a lot of dough," elucidated Denny Laine, "and only Denny Seiwell agreed with the amount offered".

As he was also amenable to uprooting to Britain, Seiwell seemed to be just what McCartney needed. As well as being an adaptable and proficient time-keeper, his blithe dedication to his craft was refreshing to Paul after the malcontented shiftlessness of certain Beatles in the months before the end.

With US guitarists Dave Spinozza and Hugh McCracken – as well as sections of the New York Philharmonic Orchestra – earning their coffee breaks with infallibly polished nonchalance, Seiwell's period in the former Beatle's employ had started with *Ram* an album that was to be attributed to "Paul and Linda McCartney". Neither presumed to dictate notes and nuances to sidemen with close knowledge of each other's considerable capabilities through working together on countless daily studio sessions, but ran through the basic essentials of every number.

The outcome was a no-frills precision that lent the majority of *Ram*'s 12 selections a dispiriting squeaky-cleanliness as if the hand-picked and highly waged players couldn't accomplish what Paul alone – for all his wispiness and casually strewn mistakes – had committed to tape instinctively on home-made *McCartney*.

This opinion was echoed also by contemporary critics with the *NME*'s "a mixed bag of psychedelic liquorice all-sorts" a prototypical reaction to the compositions *per se*. In what amounted to a personal attack, the now-radical *NME* also denigrated the McCartneys as a smug, bourgeois couple who had been too long and maybe guiltily detached from the everyday ennui of the ever-lengthening dole queues in 1970s Britain.

Yet a public that didn't read the music press were willing to assume that *Ram* and its spin-off singles would grow on them like most of *Sgt Pepper* had after repeated listening. Raw fact is that *Ram* topped the UK album list, though 'Back Seat Of My Car' struggled wretchedly to the edge of the Top 40. That *Ram* stalled at second place in Billboard's Hot 100 was mitigated by its US-only 45, 'Uncle Albert/Admiral Halsey' – freighted with sound effects and stiff-upper-lip vocal – going all the way, despite *Rolling Stone* dismissing the album as "the nadir of rock".

Comparisons of Paul's output with that of his former creative confrère were inevitable, and the conclusion of the record industry illuminati was that Lennon was cool and McCartney wasn't. Because of a cathartic projection of himself as 'Working Class Hero' on raw and intense *John Lennon: Plastic Ono Band*, Lennon was an executant of "rock" – which only the finest minds could appreciate – while McCartney peddled ephemeral "pop".

Matters didn't improve with the issue of *Wild Life*, Wings's maiden album, in time for 1971's Christmas sell-in. Four months earlier, engineer Tony Clarke had come to the Mull of Kintyre farmhouse to assist on tracks that were recorded as soon as they'd been routined. What struck him was how much was accomplished in one day compared to the months of remakes, jettisoned tracks and trifling mechanical intricacies that had to be endured from others. Understanding that it was the margin of error that had put teeth into *McCartney*, if not *Ram*, Paul was jaded with endless multi-track mixing, and made transparent his desire for *Wild Life* to be as belligerently "live" as possible – no arguments, no needless messing about with dials – and on to the next track.

However, for all its brisk finesse, *Wild Life* stalled on the edge of the Top Ten in both Britain and the USA – a tangible comedown by previous commercial standards. It was even less of a critical success than *Ram*, asking for trouble as it did with a capricious revival of The Everly Brothers' 'Love Is Strange' from 1965, and so-so originals that were also pounced upon as symptoms of creative bankruptcy. After a decade on the run – of snatched meals, irregular sleep, and pressure to come up with the next Number One – who could blame McCartney for resenting anyone who begrudged a back-street lad who'd climbed to the top of the heap, letting go, stopping trying to prove himself?

"I think I've got some idea of the way he feels about things," reckoned Denny Laine, "because I've been through the same stuff myself. The longer you go on, the tougher it is in lots of ways. People expect more and more of you. For Paul, having been part of the best rock 'n' roll band in history, it must be very heavy. I admire him so much, the way he handles it and doesn't let it interfere with his music."

"I just don't know how he does it," gasped Linda, but, to paraphrase Mandy Rice-Davies, she would say that wouldn't she? A disaffected listener's angle might be that

McCartney, *Ram* and *Wild Life* weren't magic, just music – though Paul seemed to have fun on them. He himself was to say of *Wild Life*, "OK, I didn't make the biggest blockbuster of all time, but I don't think you need that all the time. *Wild Life* was inspired by Dylan, because we'd heard that he just took one week to do an album. So we thought, 'Great, we'll do it a bit like that, and we'll try to get just the spontaneous stuff down and not be too careful with this one.' So it came out like that, and a few people thought we could have tried a bit harder."

In retrospect, nevertheless, *Wild Life*, if skimpy rather than grippingly slipshod, was enjoyable enough after the manner you'd expect from an album that, like Kingsize Taylor's Hamburg long-player, had taken three days to create from plug-in to final mix – and even 'Bip Bop', *Wild Life* at its most inconsequential, was to make more rock 'n' roll sense when Wings oozed rather than exploded onto the stage after a launch party at the Empire Ballroom, Leicester Square, London on 8 November 1971.

A small army of Paul's famous friends – Elton John, Keith Moon, Ronnie Wood of The Faces, all the usual shower – rallied round for the celebration. Paul's new hand-made suit hadn't been quite ready that afternoon, but he wore it anyway with the tracking stitches for all to see. Perhaps it was an art statement, like. Maybe the entire evening was. Most conspicuously, the entertainment laid on was nowhere to be found on the map of contemporary rock. Seated on the Empire podium was tuxedoed Ray McVay and his Dance Band, lifted by time machine from the pre-Presley 1950s. Their duties included accompanying a formation dance team; inserting rumbles of timpani at moments of climax during a grand prize raffle, and providing a framework for those who wished to hokey-cokey the night away or pursue romance to lushly orchestrated stardust-and-roses ballads.

Seizing the opportunity to rewind his life in another respect too, Paul had decided that Wings were to re-enter the concert arena with small, unpublicised, even impromptu engagements now that nearly all the essential elements were intact to enable Wings to tread the boards.

Largely through Denny Laine's urging, another guitarist was roped in. Born and raised in Londonderry, Henry McCullough had, in 1966, thrown in his lot with The People, a combo of psychedelic kidney from Portadown. Being enormous in Northern Ireland wasn't, however, enormous enough, and the group migrated to London where they were renamed Eire Apparent after being taken on by Chas Chandler, now devoting his energies to behind-the-scenes branches of the music business. As he also had The Jimi Hendrix Experience on his books, Chandler was in a strong position to obtain both a contract for Eire Apparent on Track, the Experience's label, and support spots to Hendrix both in Britain and the USA. Moreover, McCullough was rated as a guitarist by the discerning Jimi, who produced an Eire Apparent album.

Obliged by visa problems to return to Ireland during an Eire Apparent trek round North America in 1968, Henry passed through the ranks of Sweeney's Men, a renowned folk rock outfit who were about to thrust tentacles into the folk circuit on the other side of the Irish Sea, notably at that summer's Cambridge Folk Festival. Founder member Johnny Moynihan recalled, "Henry put funk into it. He'd just pick up on traditional tunes and they would come out in his playing. One night, we were playing in Dublin, and after the gig, Henry jumped in a car and drove like mad to catch the end of a John Mayall concert elsewhere. This told us what direction he was heading in, and when he was offered a job with Joe Cocker, he took it."

McCullough's arrival in Cocker's Grease Band coincided with Denny Cordell's production of the group's 'With A Little Help From My Friends' wrenching Mary Hopkin from Number One in November 1968. He was backing Joe still when the grizzled Yorkshireman was acclaimed by the half-million drenched Americans who'd braved Woodstock, viewed from a distance of decades as the climax of hippy culture. For Henry, any Woodstock euphoria was blunted when Cocker ditched the Grease Band to tour the States as *de jure* leader of retinue known as Mad Dogs And Englishmen.

Henry fell on his feet with Wings for all Cocker producer Denny Cordell's reservations: "When he played well, Henry was a genius, but he could only play in one certain bag, and you had to get him just right. Otherwise, he was very mercurial. He'd just fall out of it."

Paul McCartney was prepared to take a chance on Henry McCullough just as he was on Linda's hit-or-miss keyboard-playing – because, so he reasoned, "Linda is the innocence of the group. All the rest of us are seasoned musicians – and probably too seasoned. Linda has an innocent approach which I like. If you talk to an artist like Peter Blake, he'll tell you how much great artists love the naivety of aboriginal paintings. Linda's inclusion was something to do with that."

As well as pre-empting punk's more studied guilelessness, Linda McCartney was, according to Eric Burdon, lead singer of The Animals, an unwitting pioneer of female visibility in mainstream rock: "I think Linda played a part in paving the way for more female performers to join the boys' club called rock 'n' roll."

For those who prized technical expertise, she served as a bad example of this, beginning with her professional concert debut on Wednesday, 9 February 1972 at the University of Nottingham. The date and venue had been chosen arbitrarily as Wings cruised by car and caravan up the spine of England the previous morning. Turning off the M1 somewhere in the Midlands, they wound up at the university campus and volunteered their services. Room was made for them to do a turn during lunch hour the next day in the student's union auditorium.

Seven hundred paid 50p admission to stand around as Wings strutted their stuff – principally olde tyme rock 'n' roll and excerpts from *Wild Life*. Permitting himself the luxury of apparent self-indulgence, Paul didn't give 'em 'Yesterday', 'Let It Be' or, indeed, any of the good old good ones from The Beatles' portfolio as he took lead vocals on everything apart from reggaefied 'Seaside Woman', penned solely by Linda. A few blown riffs, flurries of bum notes, vaguely apocalyptic cadences and yelled directives – mainly at Linda – were reported, but pockets of the audience felt a compulsion to dance to Paul McCartney's first performance on a bona fide stage since Candlestick Park.

Similar casual and unannounced bashes – mostly at other colleges – filled the calendar for the next fortnight. By the final date in Oxford, Linda was solidly at the music's heart, and, for the most part, it had been an agreeable jaunt for a Paul McCartney unbothered by keening feedback bleeps, one of the sound crew blundering on to sort out a dead amplifier, a mistimed falling curtain, audience interruptions or anything else that wasn't in a slap-dash script. Either on piano or at the central microphone too, he'd been joking and swapping banter during proceedings that were epitomised by an amused cheer on the second night – in York – when Linda, crippled with nerves, forgot her cliff-hanging organ introit to *Wild Life*'s title track. Response generally was as heartening as might be expected from crowds enjoying both an unexpected diversion from customary mid-term activities and a surge into the bar afterwards, having participated, however passively in the proverbial "something to tell your grandchildren about".

13 "Mary Had A Little Lamb"

Since their manager's death, the sundering of The Beatles and the formation in 1969 of what was to become McCartney Productions and then MPL Communications, whether he made wise or foolish executive decisions, Paul alone would accept responsibility for them. However, taking care of much McCartney business were Eastman and Eastman Inc, a relationship based not so much on profit as family affinity – and friendship, particularly with brother-in-law John Eastman.

In 1972, the most immediate concern of McCartney's financiers was the mercantile possibilities of Wings's follow-up to *Wild Life*. With this in mind, stadium managers from every major territory were on the line to McCartney Productions, yelling "Klondike!" at the prospect of a round-the-world carnival of Beatles-sized magnitude.

The only snag was that the heavyweight wouldn't fight – well, not for the world championship – yet. As he had with that first low-key sweep round England with Wings, Paul not so much plunged headfirst as dipped a toe *sur le continent* with mainly 3,000 rather than 20,000 seaters over seven summer weeks that covered France to Germany, Switzerland to Finland. Wings were received with affection for what onlookers now understood they ought to expect. The set was longer and, as instanced by a projected array of rural, coastal and lunar scenes on a backcloth during the second half, more elaborate than before. Nevertheless, with the 'Long Tall Sally' encore the only nod towards The Beatles, the audiences heard much the same as their British counterparts plus sides of two recent singles and two singles yet to come.

First up had been 'Give Ireland Back To The Irish'. Perhaps not really by coincidence, John Lennon had just recorded 'Sunday Bloody Sunday', an album track which was also inspired by the bomb-blasting, bullet-firing malevolence in Northern Ireland rearing up again with the incident in Londonderry that January when 13 were shot dead by British soldiers during a civil rights demonstration. Paul's doctrinal statement about the Troubles topped the hot-blooded Irish lists, while struggling elsewhere in the teeth of radio bans and restrictions, even with an alternative instrumental version on the flip-side.

To redress the balance, Wings followed through with 'Mary Had A Little Lamb' – yes, the nursery rhyme – which, like the National Anthem, turned out to have verses other than the one everyone knew. "It wasn't a great record," confessed McCartney – and in this, he was at one with nearly all reviewers, even if, aided by four contrasting promotional shorts, it rose higher in the domestic chart than its predecessor.

"I like to keep in with the five-year-olds," he beamed, but, six months later, what did this corner of the market make of 'Hi Hi Hi', which was excluded from prudish airwaves for sexual insinuation. Yet, partly because disc-jockeys began spinning the perky, reggaefied B-side, 'C Moon', 'Hi Hi Hi' was Wings's biggest British hit thus far, going flaccid at Number Three as 1972 mutated into 1973.

The new year got underway with the UK issue of syrupy 'My Love', a taster for a forthcoming album. If sent on its way with the expected critical rubbishings, the single would be a US Number One whilst just scraping into the domestic Top Ten. Paul's status as a non-Beatle as much as that as a former Beatle was further confirmed by a *Melody Maker* journalist's random survey among schoolgirls shuffling into the Bristol Hippodrome, the first stop on Wings's first official tour of Britain that May. "What's your favourite Paul McCartney song?" "Dunno," replied one moon-faced female before pausing and adding, "Oh yeah – 'My Love'."

No longer the dream lover of old, he had emerged as a cross between admired elder brother, favourite uncle – and, for some, a character from *The Archers*, BBC Radio Four's long-running rustic soap opera. If he wasn't living the so-called "simple life" after he'd moved to East Sussex, he was living it hundreds of miles away on his farm in Scotland.

He, Linda and the girls seemed the very epitome of domestic bliss while they trod the backwards path towards the morning of the Earth.

While Rye's most renowned addressee was commuter-close to McCartney Productions, only the odd flight overhead from Gatwick airport miles away need remind him of what was over the hills in London, New York and Hollywood. It had left its mark on Paul's songwriting already – in, for example, 'Heart Of The Country' on *Ram*, and would continue to do so in the likes of the imminent 1973 B-side 'Country Dreamer' – actually taped in one of his backyards – and, most memorably of all, 1977's 'Mull Of Kintyre'.

Shrouded by meadows, greenery, exposed oak rafters, stone-flagged floors and Peace in the Valley, Paul had been all for the quietude and fresh air. Whereas they might have pressed ivory or fret, the 31-year-old musician's fingers became hardened from fencing, logging and moving bales. The most exciting daily excursion was the uncomplicated ritual of shopping for groceries as Paul and Linda became an everyday sight, hand in hand around the parish. Soon he was chatting about field drainage, nativity plays, winter farrowing and muck-spreading with the best of them – as demonstrated by him kicking up a fuss when Hibernian stag hunters presumed it was OK to cross his land, and a less justifiable one when staff at the junior school that his children attended joined a national teachers' strike in November 1986; his disapproval immortalised by one lucky amateur photographer whose back view of a McCartney stamping off in a pique across the playground, front-paged *The Times Educational Supplement*.

Nevertheless, as his home studio wasn't yet up to recording a group, he chose to fashion most of the second Wings album, *Red Rose Speedway*, in no less than five different metropolitan locations including Abbey Road. No spectator sport, the recordings themselves were only the most expensive part of a process that, before session time was even pencilled in, had started with Paul rehearsing the material with un-*Wild Life*-like exactitude, balancing ruthless efficiency with the old sweetness-and-light. Titles like 'Big Barn Red' and 'Little Lamb Dragonfly' were reflective of the maturing McCartney family's rural contentment, and a confirmation that Paul's capacity for "granny music" was bottomless. *Rolling Stone* judged *Red Rose Speedway* to be "rife with weak and sentimental drivel".

But, how could *Rolling Stone*, the *NME* and the like turn their noses up at a disc that in the USA spent a month at Number One? It may have afforded McCartney a wry grin when 'My Love' was brought down at the end of June by George Harrison's 'Give Me Love', but that lasted only a week before the latest by Billy Preston took over. Ringo's turn would come during the autumn when 'Photograph' climbed to the top of that same Hot 100. He did it again – just – in January when his "You're Sixteen" ruled pop for seven glorious days. Before the year was out, John Lennon would stick it out for a week up there too with 'Whatever Gets You Thru The Night' – and so would Wings with 'Band On The Run'.

14 "Crossroads"

The Wings show that crossed Britain in summer 1972 passed without incident other than a road manager bringing on a birthday cake for Denny Seiwell at Newcastle City Hall where the bill-toppers were joined for the encore by support act Brinsley Schwartz, harbingers of the pub-rock movement.

In the first instance, Wings too had been a reaction against the distancing of the humble pop group from its audience. Empathy with ordinary people going about their business did not extend, however, to police who had appeared backstage after a performance in Gothenberg the previous August. It had come to their ears that controlled substances, to wit 200g (7oz) of marijuana, had been discovered in a package from Britain addressed to McCartney. The tedious wheels of the Swedish legal process had been set in motion, and fines had to be paid before Wings could continue with dates in Denmark, the next country on the itinerary.

Paul passed this off as a farthing of life's small change, even hurling a metaphorical stone after his prosecutors by confiding to a journalist's cassette recorder that he intended to smoke some more of the stuff as soon as the opportunity arose. Such insolence may have provoked the unwelcome interest of the constabulary local to Campbeltown, who, visiting High Park for a routine check on the absent owner's security arrangements, recognised cannabis plants, cultivation of which was counter to the provision of the 1966 Dangerous Drugs Act, section 42.

Interrupting work on a forthcoming ITV special entitled *James Paul McCartney* to answer the summons, the McCartneys were free to go after coughing up £100. A few hours later, he was back in London, focussing his attention once again on *James Paul McCartney*. While *Melody Maker* sneered at the "overblown and silly extravaganza", it was to run a two-part feature, obsequiously headlined "Wings – Anatomy Of A Hot Band", after according the ensemble's third album, *Band On The Run*, and the single that preceded it, 'Live And Let Die', grudging praise.

Melody Maker noted too the involvement of George Martin in 'Live And Let Die', the first time he'd worked with McCartney – or any Beatle – since *Abbey Road*. The song had been commissioned as the theme for the James Bond flick of the same name and was nominated for an Oscar after almost-but-not-quite reaching Number One in the US. While 'My Love' had demonstrated that chart supremacy could give false impression of Wings's standing with the critics, 'Live And Let Die' cut the mustard, and, for the time being, most of them let McCartney in from the cold. They also listened sympathetically to *Band On The Run*, a combination of force and melody that yielded hit singles in 'Helen Wheels' (a track remaindered from the UK pressing), 'Jet' and its complex and million-selling title track.

Because Paul's favourite Studio Two at Abbey Road had been block-booked already, Wings had chosen to record the album at the only other EMI complex then available – in Lagos, Nigeria – and, even then, they were obliged to transfer to the same city's ARC Studios and endure the scowling disapproval of hired local musicians who resented what they'd perceived as non-African pop stars "plundering" the continent's musical heritage. As well as being accused unfairly of cultural burglary, the McCartneys were mugged in broad daylight by the occupants of a kerb-crawling car not long after Paul had been poleaxed by a respiratory complaint.

It never rains but it pours, and there'd been something rotten in the state of Wings before they'd so much as booked the flight from London. It had set in when Henry McCullough slumped into a glowing huff over what McCartney remembered as "something he really didn't fancy playing". This was symptomatic of a general antipathy felt by both McCullough and Denny Seiwell towards the group's music, Linda's keyboard abilities and some of the antics in *James*

Paul McCartney. Since *Wild Life*, the poisoning of Wings's reputation by pens dipped in vitriol didn't help either.

Five days after the guitarist had resigned by telephone, Seiwell threw in the towel too, mere hours before the rest left for Africa, where the troubled making of *Band On The Run* had continued with Denny Laine and, especially, Paul often finding themselves with headphones on, playing an unfamiliar instrument. Yet from the internal ructions, the tension-charged atmospheres, the drifting from pillar to post, from studio to unsatisfactory studio, surfaced the first Wings album that was both a commercial and critical triumph, back and forth at Number One at home and the Hot 100.

The release of the album and its singles hadn't been accompanied by a tour of any description, simply because Wings didn't have the personnel then. Therefore, before they could hit the road again, a search began for a replacement guitarist and drummer. An advertisement for one in the music press burst a dam on a deluge of hopefuls. To accommodate those on a short-list, Paul rented London's Albury Theatre, and hired an existing group to play four numbers with every contender while he, Denny and Linda listened in the dusty half-light beyond the footlights.

It was a long and sometimes mind-stultifying chore that led McCartney, 50 drummers later, to conclude that "I don't think auditions are much use. We won't do it again, but it was quite an experience: 50 different drummers playing 'Caravan' [a mainstream jazz standard]." Yet Paul saw it through to the bitter end, pruning the list down to five, who were to sit in with Wings. Then there were two to be each subjected to a full day – that included an interrogatory dinner – with their prospective colleagues.

There was nothing to suggest that 31-year-old Geoff Britton wasn't the *beau ideal*. He was versatile enough to have coped with stints in both rock 'n' roll revivalists, The Wild Angels and East Of Eden, one of Britain's most respected executants of jazz-rock. Geoff's black belt in karate had been a reassuring asset at the more unrefined engagements that either of these groups played.

Yet, the pop equivalent of the chorus girl thrust into a sudden starring role, Geoff turned out to be living evidence of McCartney's "I don't think auditions are much use". For a start, he was at loggerheads almost immediately with both Denny Laine and the new guitarist, Jimmy McCulloch, a Glaswegian whose *curriculum vitae* embraced stints with Thunderclap Newman – the entity responsible for anthemic 1969 UK chart-topper 'Something In The Air' – and John Mayall and Stone The Crows, fronted by Maggie Bell, a sort of Scottish Janis Joplin. The group was, however, on its last legs, and Jimmy had been one of Blue, a nice-little-band connected genealogically with Marmalade, when, on the recommendation of Denny Laine, a friend of several years standing, he was invited to play on 'Seaside Woman' (to be issued as a pseudonymous Linda McCartney single). After he gave as creditable a performance on a Mike McGear solo album at Strawberry Studios in Stockport, Jimmy became a member of Wings in June 1974.

With the group seemingly reconstituted, the McCartneys announced that dates were being pencilled in for a tour of ten countries. This, they said, was intended to last over a year, albeit with breaks lengthy enough for the making of an album to follow another one that would be out prior to the first date.

Fans from Bootle to Brisbane were on stand-by to purchase tickets, but the interval between Paul and Linda's proclamation and the opening night (at the Southampton Gaumont not quite a year later) was long enough for many to wonder if the tour was ever going to happen.

The most pressing hindrance was centred on the apparently irresolvable antagonism between Britton on the one hand and McCulloch and his less expendable pal Laine on the other. So far, Geoff had kept his fists, if not his emotions, in check, but breaking point wasn't far away. Perhaps a punch-up might have cleared the air. Nevertheless, during sessions in New Orleans's Sea Saint Studios for Wings's fourth album, *Venus And Mars*, McCartney cut the Gordian knot by finding a drummer who'd get on better with Denny and Jimmy.

The job went to Joe English, a New Yorker who had been summoned to assist on *Venus And Mars*, following Geoff Britton's crestfallen return to England. Like Denny Seiwell before him, Joe was, by his own admission, "on the bottom". This had followed six years of vocational contentment as one of Jam Factory, a unit that had criss-crossed North America, second-billed to the likes of Jimi Hendrix, The Grateful Dead and Janis Joplin. He took up the post with Wings in time for the unleashing of *Venus And Mars* and its first single, 'Listen To What The Man Said', in May 1975.

Because *Band On The Run* had been deemed a commendable effort, both were guaranteed a fair hearing by reviewers – and sufficient advance orders to slam the album straight in at Number One in every chart that mattered. 'Listen To What The Man Said' also went to the top in the States, but, true to what was becoming a precedent, fell slightly short of that in Britain. The 'Letting Go' follow-up traced a similar scent in macrocosm, nudging the US Top 40 while stopping just outside it at home. By a law of diminishing returns, however, a third A-side, 'Venus And Mars' itself, actually climbed higher than 'Letting Go' in the States while missing completely at home, becoming McCartney's first serious flop since The Beatles.

This was but a petty dampener on the overall success of an album that the majority of listeners judged to be pleasant enough, but something of a holding operation, for all its vague star-sign "concept", complete with a *Sgt Pepper*-esque reprise of the opening track, and the penultimate 'Lonely Old People' – them again – linked to a jaw-dropping version of the contrapuntal theme to *Crossroads*, the long-running ITV soap opera, set in a Midlands hotel and then broadcast during forlorn afternoon hours between the *News In Welsh* and the children's programmes – and, surmised McCartney, "just the kind of thing lonely old people watch".

It had been decided too that the two colours and two orbs that dominated the album sleeve, were to be a recurring image in both the tour merchandise and the costumes worn on a carpeted stage in the midst of scenery sufficiently minimal and plain to accommodate back-projections such as the one for 'C Moon' – a reproduction of one of the Magritte paintings Paul had been collecting since 1966. This one depicted a candle with the moon where a flame ought to be.

Between the Australian and European legs of the tour, the dramatis personnae convened at Abbey Road to get to grips with *Wings At The Speed Of Sound*, another good rather than great album, on which Paul's delegation of artistic responsibility extended as far as featuring Joe English as lead singer on 'Must Do Something About It' – while Linda's soprano was to the fore on 'Cook Of The House'. As on *Venus And Mars*, Denny and Jimmy were permitted one each. Paul, nevertheless, was loud and clear on the attendant hits, 'Let 'Em In' – and the rather self-justifying 'Silly Love Songs', which, like the album, shot to the top in the USA, Number Two in Britain.

During this and other lay-offs during the tour, the man that *Melody Maker* had front-paged lately as "Just An Ordinary Superstar" made time to attend to MPL, now the largest independent music publisher in the world with 'Happy Birthday To You', 'Chopsticks' – the most recognised (and irritating) piano solo ever composed – and key Broadway musicals amongst its litter of lucrative copyrights.

Of more personal import, however, were the US rights to Buddy Holly's best-known songs. The 40th anniversary of the bespectacled Texan's birth was marked by the first of McCartney's yearly Buddy Holly Weeks in London. Beginning on 7 September 1976 – midway between two months in the USA and the tour ending as it had begun in Britain – it climaxed with a showbiz luncheon at which guest of honour Norman Petty, Holly's studio mentor, presented a startled Paul with the cuff-links that, so he told the watching throng, had been fastening Buddy's shirt when his corpse was carried from the wreckage of the crashed aircraft.

Later celebrations – in other cities too – would embrace concerts by what was left of The Crickets; rock 'n' roll dance exhibitions; Buddy Holly painting, poetry and songwriting competitions; the opening of a West End musical about him; a "rock 'n' roll Brain Of Britain" tournament – and song contests, although the 1996 winners (a trio with a jungle-techno crack at 'Not Fade Away') at the finals in London's Texas Embassy Cantina had some of their thunder stolen by an "impromptu" jam fronted by Gary Glitter, Dave Dee, Allan Clarke of The Hollies, Dave Berry and – you guessed it – Paul McCartney.

Back in 1976, however, McCartney's primary Holly-associated concern was supervising *Holly Days* on which Denny Laine paid his respects over an entire album. But nothing from *Holly Days* was trotted out when the tour resumed or on in-concert *Wings Over America*, said to have shut down George Harrison's *All Things Must Pass* and his

Concerts For Bangla Desh as the biggest-selling triple-album of all time. Moreover, in among its reminders of Wings and the solo McCartney's chart strikes were ambles as far down memory lane as 'Yesterday', 'Lady Madonna', the White Album's 'Blackbird', and, restored to its raw pre-Spector state, 'The Long And Winding Road' off *Let It Be*. Paul seemed, therefore, to be coming to terms with both his past and present situation as he conducted Wings with nods and eye contact while never sacrificing impassioned content for technical virtuosity. As codas died away or as someone wrapped up a particularly bravura solo, he'd direct the adulation of the hordes towards others under the spotlight, and beam as salvos of clapping recognition undercut, say, the opening chords of Denny's 'Go Now'.

Ultimately, Paul McCartney had ensured that his Wings gave the people what they seemed to want – and the consensus in North America was that he'd put forward a better show than George Harrison, whose trek round the sub-continent late the previous autumn had also contained a quota of Beatles numbers among the solo favourites. John Lennon had attended a couple of George's troubled concerts, trooping backstage afterwards to say hello and ask if George had heard this rumour that at least three out of four ex-Beatles were caving in to overtures to do it all again for either a charity or some individual with more money than sense.

"God, it's like asking Liz Taylor when she's going to get together with Eddie Fisher again," Linda cracked back at another broken-record enquiry on the subject – because neither wild horses nor net temptations that worked out at hundreds of thousands of dollars per minute each for just one little concert could drag the old comrades-in-arms together again. Nevertheless, McCartney had telephoned Lennon and caught himself asking if John wanted to lend a hand on *Venus And Mars*. John didn't materialise, but Paul did for an evening of coded hilarity and nostalgic bonhomie at the open house that was a well-appointed beach villa in Santa Monica where John was living during a 15-month separation from Yoko.

Lennon and McCartney, however, finished on a sour note on Sunday 25 April 1976 when Paul returned unexpectedly, guitar in hand, to a harassed John's New York apartment after spending the previous evening there. "That was a period when Paul just kept turning up at our door. I would let him in, but finally I said to him, 'Please call before you come over. It's not 1956 [sic] anymore. You know, just give me a ring.' That upset him, but I didn't mean it badly."

Without formal goodbyes, the two friends went their separate ways, and were never to speak face-to-face again. How could either have guessed that John had less than five years left?

Wings would be over too by then. Indeed, Jimmy McCulloch and Joe English hadn't stuck around long enough to be heard on the most memorable British hit by a group, that, by autumn 1977, was pared down to just the McCartneys and Denny Laine.

15 "Japanese Tears"

In the mid-1970s, Paul McCartney's public – in Britain anyway – was comparable to that of a recurring ITV advertisement. There he was with Linda in a comedy sketch on *The Mike Yarwood Show*; grinning and facing the lens in an after-hours cluster of small-talking luminaries at a Rod Stewart concert at London's Olympia, and sharing a joke with Mick Jagger when the Stones appeared at 1976's Knebworth Festival. The McCartneys' pre-recorded personal greetings punctuated the in-person funny stories from the past when Liverpool boxing champion John Conteh – pictured with Kenny Lynch, Christopher Lee and other worthies on the front cover of *Band On The Run* – was subject of an edition of *This Is Your Life*.

More pragmatically, Paul seemed to be omnipresent on *Top Of The Pops*. As well as miming this or that latest single in an official capacity, there were on-camera sightings of him and his wife jigging about amongst the studio audience. Amused by the memory, presenter Simon Bates would reconjure "one occasion when I was on, and, of all people, Paul McCartney strolled on to the stage. Now this is totally live, and he said, 'Hi, Simon. I'm here to plug my new record.' It was the first time in a long time that a Beatle [sic] had appeared live on the show."

Maybe Paul only seemed to put in an appearance every time you switched on prime-time television, simply because there were so many sit-coms at the time with central characters that looked just like him: John Alderton in *Please Sir*, acrylically garbed Richard O' Sullivan (in *Man About The House* and *Robin's Nest*), the late Richard "Godber" Beckinsale in *Porridge*. Muddling through a weekly half-hour in, perhaps, a classroom, shared flat or, in Beckinsale's case, prison, all sported the neat, dark-haired mop-top, clean-shaven face and aspects of the chirpy persona that was the public image of "Fab Macca", who was, he declared to a waiting press corps, "over the moon" about the birth of his and Linda's first son – James – on 12 September 1977.

Elsewhere, however, it was far from fond smiles and baby-talk. Jimmy McCulloch resigned from Wings in September 1977, just prior to their knuckling down to a new album, *London Town,* while Joe English, tiring of "months and months sitting in recording studios", waiting his turn to drum, weighed up his self-picture as a musician and the cash benefits of being the last among unequals – behind Paul, Denny and one he considered a poor vocalist and keyboard player – in a group infinite numbers of rungs higher than Jam Factory had ever been.

Joe's decision to slip his cable during sessions for *London Town* seemed justified in the aftershock of *Rolling Stone*'s condemnation of the finished product as "fake rock, pallid pop and unbelievable homilies that's barely listenable next to Wings's best work," and no less an authority than Gerry Marsden shrugging off the single that followed, 'Mull Of Kintyre', with "I've never heard such a load of crap in my life." Taking to heart less reactions like this than someone's conjecture that most North Americans wouldn't know what this "mull of kintyre" meant, let alone be able find it on a map, McCartney promoted its coupling, 'Girls' School', as the A-side in the States, where it crawled to a modest Number 33.

Yet, as much co-writer Denny Laine's baby, this eulogy to Paul's Hebridean abode was a howling domestic success, replete as it was with the pentatonic skirling of a Scottish pipe band to stoke up a seasonal flavour in keeping with its release in time for 1977's December sell-in. Milkmen from Dover to Donegal whistled it, and there was no finer rendition of 'Mull Of Kintyre' than by a nine-year-old schoolboy named Matthew who, at a fête I attended in a south Oxfordshire village the following spring, clambered onto the makeshift stage, lowered the microphone and delivered it *a cappella* in an impromptu but pitch-perfect treble.

A man's gotta do what a man's gotta do. For Wings themselves, such as they were, plugging 'Mull Of Kintyre'

via both a promotional film on location in – you guessed it
– and slots on Yuletide TV variety and chat shows, was all
in a day's work until well into January. Yet while Paul was
thus mutating into as much of a British showbiz evergreen
as Max Bygraves, he was to be the only ex-Beatle to figure
still in *Melody Maker*'s yearly poll.

London Town also fared better commercially than
contemporaneous offerings by both George Harrison and
Ringo Starr. As for John Lennon, he had, to all intents and
purposes, thrown in the towel since the birth of his and Yoko's
only surviving child in 1975, seemingly rounding off his post-
Beatles career that October with a self-explanatory "best of"
retrospective, *Shaved Fish (Collectable Lennon)*.

Paul succumbed too with 1978's *Wings Greatest,* a
compilation containing his smashes as a non-Beatle up to
and including 'Mull Of Kintyre'. By its very nature, it showed
up *London Town*, still only a few months old, in an even
poorer light, despite the second of its singles, 'With A Little
Luck' tramping a well-trodden path to the top in the Hot
100 and slipping quietly in and out of the Top Ten at home.

It had been preceded by 'Goodnight Tonight', a hit 45
that, like 'Mull Of Kintyre', had nothing to do with either
London Town or the work-in-progress on the next album,
Back To The Egg. It was also among the first Wings tracks
to feature two new full-time members.

Both were more steeped in all things Beatles than anyone
who had gone before. Laurence Juber had started to learn the

guitar seriously only after hearing 'I Want To Hold Your Hand', while the first LP that drummer Steve Holly bought was *Sgt Pepper's Lonely Hearts Club Band*. The enthusiasm of these tractable young men was matched by skills acquired mostly on the London studio circuit where they'd crossed paths with Denny Laine. Consequently, each had been procured in summer 1978 by Denny for executive approval by Paul.

Neither minded being indiscernibly audible on the *Back To The Egg* session for 'Rockestra Theme' and 'So Glad To See You Here', preserved on celluloid because of arrangements that Cecil B de Mille might have approved had he been a late 1970s record producer with the run of Abbey Road and with the biggest names in British rock only a telephone call away. Led Zeppelin's John Bonham alone sent the console's decibel metre into the red, but he was but one-sixth of a percussion battalion that also included Speedy Acquaye and, from The Small Faces, Kenney Jones. Fingering unison riffs on electric guitars were Denny, Laurence, Pete Townshend, Hank B Marvin and Pink Floyd's Dave Gilmour while even Bonham's Led Zeppelin cohort, John Paul Jones, one of no less than three bass players, fought to be heard amid the massed guitars, drums, keyboards and horns.

While they made outmoded monophonic Dansette record-players shudder, the two items weren't the flat-out blasts you may have imagined on top-of-the-range stereo. They held their own, however, on *Back To The Egg*, but that isn't saying much as the album for all its diversity was subjected to a critical mauling as vicious as that for *London Town*. If none of them, in their heart-of-hearts, expected it to be astounding, the faithful bought enough copies of lacklustre *Back To The Egg* to push it into Top 20's, home and abroad, but the singles, 'Old Siam Sir' and the double A-side, 'Getting Closer' and 'Baby's Request' snatched but the slightest chart honours.

Yet mean-minded critics, flop singles, the turnovers of personnel, the eternities in the studio, none of that mattered when Wings forthcoming tour of Britain had sold out. Up there on stage at this Gaumont or that Odeon was Paul's reward for working so hard: the acclamation of the great British public. That was better than any filthy lucre or rotten review.

As the artificial show cascaded during 'Wonderful Christmastime', the latest single, he was in his element. The here and now was too important – and magical – to worry about what the *NME* had printed about *Back To The Egg*. He had the people eating out of his palm in the way he'd imagined when in a brown study during physics at the Institute.

He didn't need Wings anymore – but perhaps he never had in the first place. No time was better for letting go of the group than after the cancellation of dates in Japan early in 1980, owing to Paul's extradition after nine days as Prisoner No 22 in a Tokyo jail after customs officials at Narita airport had instructed him to open his suitcase.

Sure enough, a polythene bag of marijuana leaped out and the culprit was handcuffed and hustled by uniformed men into custody. "PAUL IN CHAINS!" screamed a headline on breakfast tables back home while the subject of the report beneath it sank into an uneasy slumber in the detention centre where the local prosecutor had demanded he be sent.

As he had after the Maharishi's tutorials in 1967, Paul insisted that he was never going to touch narcotics again, whilst either continuing or resuming his habit – as demonstrated by two related if minor run-ins with the law in 1984 when he and Linda were reprimanded and made to pay fines as inappreciable as the amounts of dope with which they'd been caught. Yet while the nasty experience in Tokyo was yet to fade, McCartney may have had every intention of staying out of trouble. "I'll never smoke pot again," he assured one British tabloid the afternoon after his inglorious farewell to the Land of the Rising Sun.

That Denny Laine – and the two new boys – had left Japan nearly a week earlier may have struck Paul as disloyal. While his glorious leader's freedom was hanging in the balance, Laine had been preoccupied with another solo album – which was to contain a single, 'Japanese Tears', an attempt to come to terms with topical events close to his heart. Issued in May, its sentiments were worthy enough, and the old conviviality between Denny, Linda and Paul hadn't dissipated immediately. Nevertheless, the seeds of Denny's departure and the subsequent demise of Wings had been sown.

16 "(Just Like) Starting Over"

As far as I'm concerned, Paul McCartney's most important contribution to society has been his very pragmatic support of animal rights. Any argument that his celebrity and wealth created the opportunity to do so is irrelevant. Others of his kind were sufficiently hip to understand that, like, cruelty to animals is wrong, and were active after a detached, sweeping, pop-starrish fashion in verbally supporting vegetarianism, anti-vivisection et al. Sometimes – because it was trendy – they'd attempted not eating meat for maybe a few weeks before the smell of frying bacon triggered a backsliding. Then they'd be noticed once again in a motorway service station, autographing a table napkin whilst masticating a pork pie or indulging in new and often disgusting passions for huntin', fishin' and shootin' with monied neighbours for whom blood sports had been second nature from childhood.

Though as much a member of the rock squirearchy as anyone else, Paul stuck at vegetarianism, following a road-to-

Damascus moment one Sunday lunchtime in the Mull of Kintyre. He was settling down to a main course of roast someone-or-other with the family whilst gazing out at an idyllic rural scene of lambs gambolling round their mothers in a meadow. After at least three decades since he pushed away his plate that day, he's still tucking into non-meat dishes exclusively, preaching the gospel of animal welfare, sinking hard cash into all manner of associated organisations, and generally keeping up the good work started by him and his first wife.

The eventual founder of a multi-national vegetarian food company, Linda's picture remains the emblem of the still-expanding, constantly improving and award-winning Linda McCartney range of products stocked in a supermarket near you. Moreover, *Linda McCartney's Home Cooking* is still the world's biggest selling recipe book of its kind.

By the final months of Wings, the catering on the road was, at Paul's insistence, entirely meat-free – though, after the lamentable incident in Tokyo, he wasn't to tour again for years, no matter how hard his various investors pleaded. Among these was CBS, who had joined the queue of major US labels supplicating him for his services as soon as executive washroom whisperings filtered through that he was about to leave Capitol. One of the hottest properties in the industry, Paul was in a position to call shots about marketing procedure. If there was the slightest deviation from the ascribed riders, wild horses wouldn't drag him out to utter one solitary syllable or sing a single note on an album's behalf.

It was a tall order, but CBS was most prepared to obey, and had also proferred the unprecedented enticement of rights to *Guys And Dolls*, *The Most Happy Fella* and further musicals containing all manner of showbiz standards by the late Frank Loesser. Thus Paul McCartney melted into CBS's caress for the next five years.

Immediately, he bounced back to Number One in the States with 'Coming Up', aided by a promotional video featuring him in various guises as every member of a band. This was an apt taster for the maiden CBS album, *McCartney II*, which returned to his solo debut's homespun and virtual one-man-band ethos.

It swept straight to the top on both sides of the Atlantic, and John Lennon grinned at his own vexation when hearing himself humming 'Coming Up' when turning a thoughtful steering wheel. Next, a personal assistant was ordered to bring him a copy of *McCartney II*. That it was such a vast improvement on the "garbage" of *Back To The Egg*, reawoke in John the old striving for one-upmanship, and was among factors that spurred a return to the studio to make his first album since reuniting with Yoko in 1975 and becoming her reclusive "househusband".

The resulting husband-and-wife effort, *Double Fantasy*, could almost be filed under "Easy Listening", but its '(Just Like) Starting Over' sold well, and, of more personal import, Paul liked 'Beautiful Boy (Darling Boy)' – track seven, side one – enough to include it among his eight choices when a "castaway" on BBC Radio Four's *Desert Island Discs* in 1982.

This lullaby to the Lennons' only child – and the album from whence it came – had been bequeathed with a "beautiful sadness" because, on 8 December 1980, two months after his 40th birthday, John Lennon had been shot dead on a New York pavement by a "fan" who was Beatle-crazy in the most clinical sense.

Accosted by a television camera crew and a stick-mike thrust at his mouth, Paul, almost at a loss for words, had uttered "It's a drag" and mentioned that he intended to carry on as intended with a day's work at a studio desk. On the printed page the next day, it seemed too blithely fatalistic, but McCartney was a shaken and downcast man, feeling his anguish all the more sharply for assuming that there'd always be another chance to talk, face each other with guitars in an arena of armchairs, and continue to bridge the self-created abyss that, in recent years, they had become more and more willing to cross. What with Wings in abeyance and John back in circulation again, the notion of Lennon–McCartney – as opposed to Lennon and McCartney – hadn't been completely out of the question.

An element of posthumous Beatlemania helped to propel 'All Those Years Ago', a vinyl salaam to Lennon by George Harrison, high up international Top 20's. A further incentive for buyers was the superimposed presence of McCartney and Wings, such as they were, who'd added their bits when the unmixed tape arrived from George's Oxfordshire mansion.

For three months, on and off, Paul and the others had been at George Martin's studio complex on Montserrat, in the distant Carribean, working on *Tug Of War*, an album that turned out to be the follow-up to *McCartney II* rather than the now-disintegrating Wings's *Back To The Egg*.

Steve Holly and Laurence Juber had had nothing to do as Paul called on more renowned if disparate helpmates such as Eric Stewart of 10cc, rockabilly legend Carl Perkins and drummer Dave Mattacks, in and out of Fairport Convention since 1969. The sessions were notable too for an artistic reunion with not only George Martin as producer, but also Ringo Starr, fresh from *Stop And Smell The Roses*, an LP with a more pronounced "famous cast of thousands" approach.

To this, Paul had donated the title track and catchy 'Attention', but had decided to cling onto another composition, 'Take It Away'. Instead, it was opening track and the fourth of no less than six singles from *Tug Of War* – which went the chartbusting way of *McCartney II*, when released in April 1982. Among other highlights were 'Here Today' – a more piquant tribute to Lennon than singalong 'All Those Years Ago' – and 1982's 'Ebony And Ivory', a duet with Stevie Wonder, which, issued on 45, was another double-first in Britain and North America.

Whereas this liaison had been instigated by Paul, he himself had been solicited by Michael Jackson who, like Wonder, was a former Tamla-Motown child star. Now chronologically adult, he had been in the throes of recording the celebrated *Thriller* in Los Angeles. Paul was among the well-known guest musicians, and 'The Girl Is Mine', his cameo as jovial voice-of-experience to Michael's cheeky young shaver, was one of its hit 45s.

McCartney was paid in kind when Jackson pitched in on 'Say Say Say' from 1983's *Pipes Of Peace*, Paul's third post-Wings album. It also contained a title track that would be its maker's commercial apotheosis in Britain during the 1980s as 'Mull Of Kintyre' had been in the previous decade. A Yuletide Number One that lingered in the Top 50 for three months, it was helped on its way by a video that re-enacted the mythical and sociable seasonal encounter in No Man's Land between British and German soldiers in World War I.

The previous month, the critics had crucified the album. Surely *Melody Maker* had mistaken *Pipes Of Peace* for *Double Fantasy*, calling it "congratulatory self-righteous" and "slushy" – while the *NME* weighed in with "a tired, dull and empty collection of quasi-funk and gooey rock arrangements". In retrospect, some of the tracks were rather in-one-ear-and-out-the-other, but, on the whole, it was pleasant enough, even if the stand-out numbers were its two singles.

The first of these, 'Say Say Say', Michael Jackson returning of the *Thriller* favour, had suffered poor reviews too, but the public thought otherwise, and it shifted millions. It helped that Jackson was still basking in the afterglow of *Thriller* to the degree that even a video about the making of the Grammy-winning album precipitated stampedes into the megastores the minute their glass doors opened.

George Harrison judged *The Making Of Michael Jackson's Thriller* "the squarest thing I've ever seen," adding, "It was a bit off the way Michael bought up our old catalogue when he knew Paul was also bidding. He was supposed to be Paul's mate."

The Beatles portfolio was to become Jackson's property for a down payment of nearly £31 million, more than McCartney could afford, when ATV, its previous publishers, were open to offers for this and other bodies of work in 1986. Neither was McCartney pleased about how 1984's self-financed and feature-length *Give My Regards To Broad Street* film was received. The initial shard of inspiration for this "musical fantasy drama" had cut him more than two years earlier during an otherwise tedious stop-start drive into rush-hour London. With a screenplay by Paul himself, the interlocking theme was a world-class pop star's search for missing master tapes for an album. There were also musical interludes of which the majority were refashionings of Beatles and Wings favourites – though 'No More Lonely Nights', an opus fresh off the assembly-line, was the attendant hit single.

Throughout the six months of shooting, Andros Eraminondas guided and tempered his endlessly inventive paymaster's designations that, to outsiders, seemed as rash as a good half of *Magical Mystery Tour* had been. Nevertheless, throughout the interminable running of each celluloid mile, McCartney had been impressive for his learned recommendations about rhythm and pacing. Yet *Variety*, the *Bible* and *Yellow Pages* of the latest cinema releases, shoved aside *Give My Regards To Broad Street* as "characterless, bloodless and pointless". As they always were, journals local to the towns where it was distributed were kinder, albeit while homing in less on the story-line than the spectacular visual effects, some of which were seen too in subsequent videos for singles such as 'Only Love Remains', the principal ballad on his next album, *Press To Play*, which was centred on two elderly actors playing some dingy couple still in love after maybe half a century of wedlock: Darby and Joan who used to be Jack and Jill.

Three years before, McCartney had addressed himself to Jack, Jill and other infant video-watchers with *Rupert And The Frog Song*, 25 minutes dominated by one of the *Daily Express* cartoon character's adventures with voiceovers by sit-com shellbacks Windsor Davis and June Whitfield plus Paul himself, who'd owned the film rights to the checked-trousered bruin since 1970. It was to defy all comers when it appeared among BAFTA nominees as 1985's "Best Animated Short Film". Proving what traditionalists toddlers are, it also topped the video charts the previous Christmas. Into the bargain, the soundtrack's principal composition, 'We All Stand Together', sung by the animated frogs, had been high in the UK Top Ten.

Was there no end to this man's talent? He popped up again at Wembley Stadium that summer, emoting a gremlin-ridden 'Let It Be' to his own piano as satellite-linked Live Aid approached its climax. Then he joined the assembled cast for a finale in which he and Pete Townshend bore organiser Bob Geldof on their shoulders.

Geldof was to be knighted for his charitable efforts. Another milestone along rock's road to respectability was the heir to the throne's Prince's Trust Tenth Birthday Gala in June 1986. Paul gave 'em 'I Saw Her Standing There' and 'Long Tall Sally' prior to closing the show by leading an omnes fortissimo 'Get Back'. A handshake from Prince Charles afterwards had less personal significance to McCartney than the fact that he'd just completed his first formal appearance in an indoor venue since Wings's last flap at Hammersmith Odeon in 1979.

If his main spot had been as nostalgic in its way as Gerry And The Pacemakers on the chicken-in-a-basket trail, in terms of audience response, he'd held his own amid Me-generation entertainers like Bryan Adams, Paul Young and, with their whizz-kid singing bass player, Level 42, not to mention Tina Turner, Eric Clapton, the ubiquitous Elton John and all the other old stagers. Like them, he couldn't take Top 40 exploits for granted anymore, but *Press To Play* hovered round the middle of most international Top 30s, and the singles made token showings in some charts, even drippy 'Only Love Remains' after it filled Paul's entire slot on 1986's *Royal Variety Command Performance*.

He had better luck both critically and commercially – in Britain certainly – with 1987's *All The Best*, his second reassemblage of selected Wings and solo. This triumph of repackaging was to be gilded months later by *Sgt Pepper Knew*

My Father on which several new acts depped for the Lonely Hearts Club Band – with Billy Bragg's 'She's Leaving Home' and Wet Wet Wet's 'With A Little Help From My Friends' as its chart-topping double A-side.

There'd be more fleeting *Top Of The Pops* visitations – either on video or in the chicken-necked flesh – with their latest releases by such young hopefuls as Cliff Richard, The Rolling Stones, The Kinks and, a week before his sudden death in 1989, Roy Orbison. As the millennium crept closer, Paul McCartney would also score to a diminishing degree, not so much with songs he could have written in his sleep, but through a combination of pulling unexpected strokes, stubbornly treading steep and rugged pathways, and otherwise maintaining a lingering hip sensibility, often justifying the words of John McNally of The Searchers: "You don't have to be young to make good records."

Even on "Sounds Of The Sixties" nights in the most dismal working men's club, The Searchers, The Troggs, Dave Berry and those of corresponding vintage would lure a strikingly young crowd by counterpoising contemporary offerings with the old showstoppers. After disappearing for years, neither was it laughable for others who'd travelled an unquiet journey to middle life to embark on sell-out trans-continental tours as did Paul Simon, Fleetwood Mac, The Grateful Dead, Leonard Cohen – and, after a decade away, Paul McCartney.

17 "Ain't That A Shame"

Present on guitar and backing vocals in *Tug Of War* and *Pipes Of Peace*, Eric Stewart had also been evident in *Give My Regards To Broad Street*. He was also on hand to sling in rhymes, chord changes and twists to the plot as McCartney pieced together possibilities for what became *Press To Play*. Musically, this album had been proficient but not adventurous.

However, many of the lodged conventions of songwriting methodology since the beat boom were thrust aside when McCartney next bonded with Elvis Costello, one of the most successful post-pub rock ambassadors to get anywhere in North America.

That 33-year-old Costello had finished his formal education in Liverpool – and spent many previous school holidays with relations there – may have been a plus point for Paul. Offering hip credibility too, Costello was just what unfashionable McCartney needed, and, after initial slight misgivings, the two buckled down to "writing a bunch of really good songs," smiled Elvis. "It was great working with him. I was thrilled."

Five hours a day in a room above Paul's studio in Sussex resulted in items for both Paul's *Flowers In The Dirt* and Declan's *Spike*. The general thrust of the McCartney–McManus output was the tempering of an abrasive edge with attractive tunes. 'My Brave Face' – a man's bitter freedom from his woman – just about reached the UK Top 20 for Paul with follow-up 'This One' touching exactly the same apogee (Number 18) but barely troubling the Hot 100 where 'My Brave Face' had got a look in at Number 25.

These so-so market volleys were incidental to *Flowers In The Dirt* returning McCartney to the top of all manner of album lists, and the ten months of the global tour earning an award from a US financial journal as the highest grossing such excursion of 1990 – with a stop in Rio de Janeiro breaking the world attendance record for a pop concert with a paying audience.

Spanning nearly every familiar trackway of Paul's career from 'Twenty Flight Rock' of Quarry Men vintage to 'My Brave Face', he was backed by quite a motley crew consisting of Linda, guitarist Robbie McIntosh (who'd quit The Pretenders during sessions for a 1986 album), keyboard player and former PE teacher Paul Wickens, drummer Chris Whitten (who'd been with Wickens in a group led by self-styled "pagan rock 'n' roller" Julian Cope) and general factotum Hamish Stuart, founder member of the Average White Band.

Stuart picked guitar very prettily on quasi-traditional 'All My Trials', an in-concert single captured in Milan. As well as filling one side of a single, it, utilised time on *Tripping The Light Fantastic*, a triple-album that was the quaint vinyl souvenir of the round-the-world expedition. Another by-product was the limited-edition *Unplugged: The Official Bootleg,* an acoustic recital after the ticket-holders shuffled in from the February chill to the relatively downhome ambience of Limehouse Studios amid London's dockland wharfs. Some would see themselves in a consequent *MTV* broadcast, the first one to be issued on a record.

The loudest ovations throughout these latest rounds of public displays would always be for the many unrevised Beatles selections. Audiences also clapped hard for Paul's olde tyme rock 'n' roll excursions. Both Eddie Cochran's 'Twenty Flight Rock' and Fats Domino's 'Ain't That A Shame' had just been recorded by Paul among items of similar vintage for *Choba B CCCP* (translated as "Back In The USSR") a Russia-only album of favourite non-originals dating from between Hitler's invasion of the Soviet Republic in 1941 and The Beatles' final season at the Star-Club in his defeated Germany.

Choba B CCCP came out just before the Berlin Wall came down in 1989. With the establishment of a Macdonald's fast-food outlet off Red Square not far away, it seemed an expedient exercise to fire a commercial broadside directly at consumers hitherto deprived of music from the very morning of post-war pop. Just as The Beatles' versions of

'Twist And Shout', 'Long Tall Sally', 'Money' et al were the only versions for anyone whose entrée to pop had been 'Please Please Me', so McCartney's would be of 13 set-works from the annals of classic rock for Russian record-buyers until they came upon the originals – and, in the late 1980s, there seemed fat chance of that for a while. Besides, as David Bowie, Bryan Ferry, The Hollies – and John Lennon – were a handful of the many who'd indulged in entire albums of oldies already, why shouldn't Paul?

His walks down memory lane also extended to disguised ambles round Liverpool. How delightful it was to mingle anonymously among shoppers in a Wavertree precinct; in a pub garden on the Cheshire plain, or browsing in a second-hand book shop up Parliament Street. He noticed that *a* Cavern had been reconstructed down Mathew Street next to Cavern Walks shopping mall. On the now-busy thoroughfare's opposite side stood the John Lennon pub and, halfway up a wall, an Arthur Dooley statue of a madonna-like figure – "Mother Liverpool" – with a plaque beneath reading "Four Lads Who Shook The World", and one of them, like, flying away with wings. Get it?

Civic pride in The Beatles had been emphasised further in 1982 by naming four streets on a housing estate after each of the four most famous members – Paul McCartney Way, Ringo Starr Drive and so forth – in spite of one disgruntled burgher's opposition "in the light of what went on in Hamburg and their use of filthy language."

While *Backbeat* – a silver screen perspective on John, Paul, George and Pete in Hamburg – loomed on the horizon, "Beatle conventions" had been fixtures in cities throughout the world for years. Frequent attractions – especially when each August's Merseybeatle festival was on – at both the new Cavern in Mathew Street and the more authentic one in the Beatles museum on Albert Dock were groups whose *raison d'être* was re-enacting some phase of The Beatles' career from the enlistment of Ringo to the end of the Swinging Sixties. Others of their ilk paid homage to solely one Beatle as did Band On The Run, Hari Georgeson, Starrtime and the short-lived Working Class Heroes. By the mid-1990s, there'd be nigh on 200 such tribute bands in Britain alone, virtually all of them encumbered with a right-handed "Paul".

While it was said that he procured one of the "Pauls" as a stand-in for a video shoot, McCartney was to raise an objection that, in *Backbeat*, "John" rather than his character sang 'Long Tall Sally', and seemed bemused generally that anyone should make a living impersonating The Beatles.

18 "Come Together"

Paul's next album, *Off The Ground* was the product of a satisfied mind. Polished and mostly unobjectionable, it was never expected to be astounding – by marginal McCartney enthusiasts anyway – but it sufficed because skillful arrangements and technological advances can help conceal mediocre songs in need of editing. It nudged the Top 20 in the USA where Beatlemania was always more virulent than anywhere else, and those afflicted bought Paul's records out of habit to complete the set like Buffalo Bill annuals. Over here, too many didn't want to like *Off The Ground*, but, as it had been in 1989, the press could slag off Paul's records; latter-day punks could denigrate him as one more bourgeois liberal with inert conservative tendencies, and hippies disregard him as a 'breadhead', but there he was again, running through his best-loved songs for the people who loved them – and him – best of all in Melbourne Cricket Ground, Louisiana Superdome, Munich's Olympiahalle and further packed-out stadia designed originally for championship sport.

As always, the mood was light, friendly, but what would have happened had the main set ended with politely brief clapping instead of the foot-stomping and howling approval that brought Paul back on for the encores of 'Band On The Run', 'I Saw Her Standing There' and, finally, everyone blasting up chorus after da-da chorus of 'Hey Jude'?

Yet, however slickly predictable his stage show was becoming, he would prove to have much in common in his way with David Bowie, Jeff Beck, Van Morrison and other advocates of the artistic virtues of sweating over something new while Elton John, Phil Collins, Stevie Wonder and like Swinging Sixties contemporaries continued cranking out increasingly more ordinary albums.

Paul got into the swing of keeping you guessing what he'll be up to next by paying close attention to what made his now-teenage children and their friends groove nowadays, and making his first and foremost essay as an exponent of the Modern Dance. He managed it in collaboration with genre producer Martin "Youth" Glover – though perhaps just in case they looked back in anger at it, McCartney and Glover hid themselves beneath a pseudonym – The Fireman – for the fusion of "downtempo house" and a vague strata of dub-reggae heard on 1993's *Strawberries Oceans Ships Forest* as well the more freeform and slow-moving ambient-techno of *Rushes* four years later.

Good old-fashioned guitars reared up among the

synthesizers and samples in *Rushes*, and the overall effect was considered tame and old-fashioned by Modern Dance connoisseurs. Nevertheless, it demonstrated that Fab Macca dug the latest sounds – just as *Liverpool Oratorio* had his appreciation of classical music. As Martin Glover was to be the catalyst for The Fireman business, so Paul had leant on Carl Davis, known chiefly as the classically trained composer of television incidental music and film scores, for this maiden venture into what he'd been brought up to regard as highbrow nonsense: "When symphonies came on the radio, my family just went, 'Oh bloody hell!' and switched the station."

After the job had been done, there was a hiccup when Paul insisted that it be officially titled *Paul McCartney's Liverpool Oratorio*, but Carl, if initially affronted, caved in, and continued kneading the work into shape for the première at Liverpool's Anglican cathedral on 28 June 1991.

BBC Music magazine opined that even its most melodic excerpts "fell short of the standards set in his finest pop tunes," and suggested that McCartney had "yet to find a distinct 'classical' voice." Nonetheless, while reaching a lowly 177 in Billboard's pop chart, the album displaced Italian tenor Luciano Pavarotti from the top of the classical list, performing similarly in Britain.

Although McCartney didn't thus reinvent himself as a sort of nuclear age Sir Arthur Sullivan by juggling milkman-friendly catchiness and Handel-like choral works, *Liverpool Oratorio* was instrumental in narrowing the gap between highbrow and lowbrow, "real" singing and "pop" caterwauling, 'La Donna E Mobile' and 'Long Tall Sally'. Pertinent to this discussion too, the University of Liverpool opened Britain's first Institute of Popular Music – with Mike McCartney among those in its working party. Was it not entirely fitting that a self-contained faculty to centralise existing work should have originated in the birthplace of The Beatles?

The same could be said of the Liverpool Institute of Performing Arts – LIPA – a notion that had come to Paul McCartney shortly before his old secondary school closed in the mid-1980s, and "this wonderful building, which was built in 1825, was becoming derelict. Various people suggested to me that I could help by taking the kids off the streets in some way. Four years ago, I announced the plan to build LIPA, and we started fund-raising. I put in some money to get it going, and we got a lot of help from different people."

It was to be, he said, "like the school in the TV series, *Fame*" in that talented youngsters could be primed for greener pastures via courses that included an artistic conditioning process that, time permitting, might involve songwriting tutorials by none other than the very founder himself – "but I won't be telling the kids how to do it because I think that it is part of my skill that I don't know exactly how to write a song, and the minute I do know how to do it, I'm finished. So I would want to explain that I don't agree that there is an accepted method of writing a song."

The Institute was to enroll its first students for 1996's spring term in between the preceding media hoo-hah that always went with the McCartney territory and the official unveiling of its plaque by the Queen – who'd been among those who'd dipped into her purse for LIPA – in June.

George Harrison's loyalty to the old grey stones was strong enough for him to reach for his cheque book on LIPA's behalf too. He had also been amenable to joining with Paul and Ringo in 1994 for the compilation of *Anthology*, a vast Beatles retrospective that would embrace eventually nine albums (in sets of three), a lengthy television documentary – later available on video and DVD – and a group autobiography in the form of edited transcripts of taped reminiscences. "There were one or two bits of tension," smiled Paul, "I had one or two ideas George didn't like." One of these was the project's working title, *The Long And Winding Road*, because it was after one of McCartney's songs. Ringo too blew hot and cold with Paul: "It's a good month and a bad month, just like a family."

Since John's passing, there'd been no successor to him as self-appointed paterfamilias, but Yoko had remained to The Beatles roughly what the embarrassing "Fergie", the Duchess of York, is to the Windsors. Yet she and Paul had shared a conciliatory hug at a Rock 'N' Roll Hall Of Fame award ceremony, and before the weather vane of rapprochement lurched back to the old thinly veiled antagonism, Yoko donated stark voice-piano tapes of Lennon compositions for

McCartney, Harrison and Starr to use as they thought fit.

Two of them, 'Free As A Bird' and 'Real Love' were transformed into successive Beatles A-sides to go with the *Anthology* merchandise. Events since have demonstrated that it was far from the last word on the group. Not a month passes without another few books adding to the millions of words chronicling and analysing some aspect or other of their history. Bootlegs have continued unabated too with their manufacturers intrigued most recently by the emergence in Holland of further hitherto-unissued unforgiving minutes from the *Let It Be* era.

Thus The Beatles endure after the apparent levelling out of Britpop from its mid-1990s apogee. While it was going strongest, as he had with the Modern Dance, Paul McCartney, well into his 50s, masticated a chunk of Britpop too by combining with 37-year old Paul Weller and, more to the point, Noel Gallagher, leader of Oasis, on an Abbey Road reworking of 'Come Together' for *Help!* a 1995 "various artists" album to raise funds to alleviate the war in Bosnia's aftermath of homelessness, lack of sanitation, disease and starvation. Symbolising three generations of pop aristocracy, the trio – naming themselves The Smokin' Mojo Filters – were *Help!*'s star turn, and, almost as a matter of course, 'Come Together' was its loss-leader of a single.

19 "Lonesome Tears"

Classical composer Sir William had been responsible too for *Fanfare For Brass* for EMI's celebration of its first 50 years in business, but for the label's centenary in 1997, Paul McCartney came up with *Standing Stone*, a symphonic poem that the sniffy *Music* periodical reckoned "represented a significant leap forward in style and substance, the persuasive outcome of almost four years labour."

His mood was one of quiet confidence when settling into a seat at the Royal Albert Hall for the London Symphony Orchestra and Chorus's première of *Standing Stone* at the Royal Albert Hall on 14 October 1997. Pockets of the audience behaved as if it was a rock concert, though they remained silent and not visibly fidgeting during the grandiloquent music that finished with "love is the oldest secret of the universe" from the choir, prefacing some ticket-holders' exclaimed "yeah!" that set off a standing ovation.

Overnight, the press gathered its thoughts. The reviews

weren't scathing, but *Standing Stone* wasn't an especially palpable hit either now that the novelty of Paul McCartney, classical composer, had faded. Nevertheless, it was received more favourably at New York's Carnegie Hall the following month in a performance that was broadcast to nigh on 400 radio stations across the whole sub-continent. Of later recitals, the most far-reaching was that on British television one Christmas morning when the nation was midway between the children's pre-dawn ripping open of the presents and the Queen's Speech.

The morning after 14 October 1997, however, the critics had tended to overlook the McCartney pieces that had prefaced the main event at the Albert Hall. These were the seven movements of 'A Leaf' and another orchestrated piece 'Spiral' – for piano – as well as 'Stately Horn' for a horn ensemble, and 'Inebriation' from The Brodsky Quartet.

Now that he'd acquired a taste for it, Paul would be knocking out more of the same, most recently *Ecce Cor Meum* – "behold my heart" – an oratorio dedicated to Linda, that was the centrepiece of the first concert given at Magdalen College, Oxford's new chapel in November 2001.

Listening to that of McCartney's classical output issued thus far on disc – which includes the 'Andante' from *Standing Stone* as a single – adjectives like "restrained", "shimmering", "caressing" and "atmospheric" occurred to me, and a lot of it has, indeed, a reposeful daintiness that's just, well, nice.

The same adjective might be applied to 1995's *Oobu*

Joobu, a radio series commissioned by the same US company that had networked the self-explanatory *Lost Lennon Tapes*. Here, Paul presided over harmless family fun with records, jingles, funny stories, celebrity interviews, comedy sketches, previously unbroadcasted Beatles and Wings tapes, you get the drift. There were also what might have been categorised in a more sexist age, "women's features" – mainly recipes – by Linda. The children, however, made only incidental contributions at most. Advisedly, they'd been so removed from direct public gaze that, as teenagers, they were able to walk around Rye and Campbeltown not unnoticed exactly, but without inviting too much comment.

Domestically, the mid-1990s would be remembered by Paul not only for what happened at the end, but also for the contentment that had preceded it. Nothing was ever the same afterwards.

Lightning struck slowly. In December 1995, Linda recovered from an ostensibly successful operation to remove a lump from her breast. Yet within weeks, she had every appearance of being seriously ill, and was prescribed chemotherapy. That held the spread of what was obviously cancer at arm's length, but X-rays were to reveal malignant cells forming a shadow on her liver.

The ghastly secret became known to a media that noted Linda's absence when Paul was driven to Buckingham Palace on 11 March 1997. As Prime Minister John Major had done on the apparent behalf of Eric Clapton MBE, Van

Morrison OBE and Sir Cliff so his more with-it successor, Tony Blair, a self-styled 'guy' had advised the Queen to invest the showbusiness legend as responsible for 'I Saw Her Standing There' as *Liverpool Oratorio* with a knighthood – for "services to music". Sir Paul McCartney then sealed his status as pillar of the Establishment by paying £3,500 for a coat of arms. Among its symbols were a guitar and two circles representing records to signify what was still his principal source of income.

To that end, *Flaming Pie*, his first non-concert album for nearly half a decade, materialised two months after the visit to the Queen. Unlike, say, *Ecce Cor Meum*, it wasn't meant to be taken especially seriously. "I called up a bunch of friends and family and we just got on and did it," he chortled. "And we had fun. Hopefully, you'll hear that in the songs."

Those that did bought *Flaming Pie* in sufficient quantity to ease it up to Number One and to Number Two in the Hot 100. This flew in the face of dejecting critiques for an album that conveyed a likeably downhome, sofa-ed ambience.

Nowhere in its lyrics was any intimation that Linda was dying by inches. More a hospital orderly than passionate inamorato now, Paul tried to blow sparks of optimism but resigned himself with wearied amazement that she was still clinging on as he helped attend to her day-long needs.

The flame was low on the evening of Thursday 16 April 1998, and 56-year-old Linda Louise McCartney was gone by the grey of morning.

20 "She Said Yeah"

Predictably, there were rumours of a lady friend within months of Linda's funeral, but there was no evidence to substantiate a new romance until late in 1999 when Paul was seen in public with a blonde from Tyne-and-Wear named Heather Mills, whose artificial leg was of no more account than an earring or a headband. On 8 August 1993, she had been knocked down by a police motorcycle, and hastened to the nearest hospital where surgeons were obliged to amputate. With extraordinary resilience, Heather Mills conquered desolation by anchoring herself to the notion that, one way or another, she'd emerge, if not entirely intact, then with hardened mettle. At least she could afford – especially with the out-of-court settlement by Scotland Yard – the thousands of pounds required for a shapely silicone limb with a flexible foot.

She also inaugurated the Heather Mills Trust, a charity for those who had become limbless in global theatres of war. Her tireless fund-raising involved a 1999 Heather Mills single entitled 'Voice' – with a lyric about a disabled girl – and spell-binding slots on chat-shows where she provoked shocked laughter by rolling up her trousers and even removing her false leg. Up in the control room, where the producer barked excited instructions to the camera operators, it was fantastic television.

It also had the desired effect of drawing attention to a campaign that was to earn Heather a Nobel Peace Prize nomination and further recognitions for her work. Famous enough to warrant a frank-and-unashamed autobiography, she was a host at one such ceremony at London's plush Dorchester Hotel. Her future husband was there too, clutching the Linda McCartney Award For Animal Welfare he was to give to the founder of Viva, an associated movement.

Taking a benevolent interest in Heather's activities, Paul McCartney was to write out a huge cheque for the trust, and contribute plucked guitar and backing vocals to 'Voice'. Then one thing led to another, and the 59-year-old widower seemed as fondly in love as he could be with a beautiful girlfriend a quarter of a century his junior.

He went public in other matters too. Three years after a Paul McCartney art exhibition opened at the Kunstforum Lyz Gallery in Hamburg on 30 April 1999, he risked a display at the Walker in Liverpool – which was also curating some Turners in an adjacent gallery. This was perhaps unfortunate in its inviting of comparisons between the distinguished Victorian "colour poet" and one who wouldn't be there if not for the Fab Four's long shadow.

While one expert deemed Paul's efforts to be "more interesting than I thought" and another in the same newspaper reckoned they had "promise", a third critic turned his nose up at "wholly talentless daubs. Perhaps endless adulation has made McCartney deaf to the voice of criticism."

Maybe the Beatles' fairy-tale had rendered this particular scribe as deaf to the voice of approbation. Either way, McCartney was in a no-win situation – unless he'd exhibited his art pseudonymously. Yet little intimates that because Paul McCartney was so fully occupied with his musical career, he was a regrettable loss to the world of fine art. As a figure in time's fabric, his period as a Beatle will remain central to most considerations of him.

He'd harked back to the years prior to the 'Love Me Do' countdown with 1999's *Run Devil Run*, a quasi-*Choba B CCCP* album, but with three originals in the same vein. Anyone with the confidence to slot these in without jarring the stylistic flow of such as 'All Shook Up', 'Brown-Eyed Handsome Man', 'She Said Yeah', and 'Blue Jean Bop' deserved attention. The most significant plug for *Run Devil Run* was an end-of-the-century bash at the replica Cavern along Mathew Street to a capacity raffle-winning crowd but with a webcast audience of over three million.

His fans loved it, but they weren't so sure about an album taped after Martin "Youth" Glover reared up again as producer of Super Furry Animals, formed in Cardiff in the mid-1990s as an amalgam of the Modern Dance, Britpop and olde tyme progressive rock. At an *NME* awards evening in February 2000, they and McCartney chatted amiably enough, and through the agency of Glover, they were to collaborate on *Liverpool Sound Collage*, which was to be up for a Grammy as 2001's "Best Alternative Musical Album". It had been intended in the first instance as an aural backdrop to "About Collage", an exhibition at the Tate Liverpool by Peter Blake, whose pop-associated pursuits had not ended with his montage for the *Sgt Pepper* front cover.

Neither had Paul's non-pop dabblings with the Walker exhibition, though he was on firmer ground with 2001's *Blackbird Singing*, a collection of over 100 poems interspersed with lyrics from some of his songs.

Over an album's worth of new compositions were dashed off in a fortnight with a guitar–keyboards–drums trio of Los Angeles session players whose keeping of expensive pace with him was leavened by technical precision deferring to spontaneity. "We didn't fuss about it," he shrugged. "I'd show them a song, and we'd start doing it." These included 'From A Lover To A Friend', the only A-side. It lasted a fortnight in the domestic Top 50, and proceeds were donated to the families of New York's fire service who perished in the aftershock of the terrorist attacks on the World Trade Center.

Paul had been present when the hijacked aeroplanes tore into the heart of the Big Apple, and had organised an all-star benefit concert at Madison Square Garden with no political agenda other than raising money for the firefighters and other victims, and to show solidarity against terrorism. Naturally, he wrote a song about it.

As a raw composition, 'Freedom' was convoluted and over-declamatory, but that didn't matter in the context of the euphoric atmosphere on that October Saturday six weeks after "nine-eleven". Nonetheless, he wasn't to perform it when he commenced what he was to call his "Back In The World" tour. Prior to setting off, however, there was something McCartney had to do that was as special in its way as the New York spectacular. In November 2001, George Harrison had died of cancer. A memorial concert took place at the Empire on what would have been his 59th birthday on 24 February 2002. Paul shared a few yarns with the audience and, at the very end, gave 'em a spirited 'Yesterday'.

He paid homage to George again on more glittering events at the Albert Hall – and on 3 June 2002 at Elizabeth II's "Jubilee Concert" in the grounds of Buckingham Palace, which reached a climax of sorts in a duet with Eric Clapton of George's 'While My Guitar Gently Weeps' from the White Album.

Not seen in the televisual coverage was the final number, 'I Saw Her Standing There'. As its coda yet reverberated, Paul was thinking ahead to the following Monday when he was to marry Heather Mills – for whom he'd penned an eponymous song on *Driving Rain* – at a castle hired for that very purpose in the Irish republic. Theirs was the fuss wedding of the year after the elderly laird, unused to press encroachment, gave the game away.

Back from the honeymoon, the groom embarked on the second leg of what was now a wartime tour. Wherever he could (on programmes or the spin-off "live" album), he ensured that composing credits read "McCartney–Lennon" like they had fleetingly before Parlophone and everyone else had made it the more alphabetically correct "Lennon–McCartney", even on the *Anthology*. Paul's attempt then to have it otherwise had been vetoed by John's volatile relict, and reawoke a dispute that hasn't yet been resolved. You can understand Paul's attitude. On the basis of mostly song-by-song breakdowns by Lennon during one of his last interviews, BBC Radio Merseyside presenter Spencer Leigh figured out that, statistically, McCartney was responsible for approximately two-thirds of The Beatles' output of originals, including 'Yesterday' and 'Hey Jude'. In a weighty press statement, Paul fulminated too that "Late one night, I was in an empty bar, flicking through the pianist's music book when I came across '"Hey Jude" written by John Lennon'. At one point, Yoko earned more from 'Yesterday' than I did."

On his 50th birthday in 1992, however, there'd been no anger but a certain melancholy as Paul mused that "despite the successful songs I've written like 'Yesterday', 'Let It Be' and 'Hey Jude', I feel I just want to write one really good song. I still have a little bee in my bonnet telling me, 'The best could be yet to come.' That keeps me going."

Songography
By Ian Drummond

All songs composed by Paul McCartney, with co-writers appearing in brackets. Listed by artist/band and then in chronological order of composition. All dates refer to album and single releases unless otherwise stated.

THE BEATLES

'In Spite Of All The Danger' (Harrison)	*Anthology 1* (Nov 1995)
'Cayenne'	
'Like Dreamers Do' (Lennon)	

'I Saw Her Standing There' (Lennon)	*Please Please Me* (Mar 1963)
'Misery' (Lennon)	
'Chains' (Lennon)	
'Ask Me Why' (Lennon)	
'Please Please Me' (Lennon)	
'Love Me Do' (Lennon)	
'PS I Love You' (Lennon)	
'Do You Want To Know A Secret?' (Lennon)	
'There's A Place' (Lennon)	

'From Me To You' (Lennon)	Single (Apr 1963)
'Thank You Girl' (Lennon)	'From Me To You' B-side (Apr 1963)

'She Loves You' (Lennon)   Single (Aug 1963)
'I'll Get You' (Lennon)   'She Loves You' B-side (Aug 1963)

'I'll Be On My Way' (Lennon)   *Live At The BBC* (Nov 1994)

'It Won't Be Long' (Lennon)   *With The Beatles* (Nov 1963)
'All I've Got To Do' (Lennon)
'All My Loving' (Lennon)
'Little Child' (Lennon)
'Hold Me Tight' (Lennon)
'I Wanna Be Your Man' (Lennon)
'Not A Second Time' (Lennon)

'I Want To Hold Your Hand' (Lennon)   Single (Nov 1963)
'This Boy' (Lennon)   'I Want To Hold Your Hand' B-side (Nov 1963)

'I Call Your Name' (Lennon)   *Long Tall Sally* EP (Jun 1964)

'A Hard Day's Night' (Lennon)   *A Hard Day's Night* (Jul 1964)
'I Should Have Known Better' (Lennon)
'If I Fell' (Lennon)
'I'm Happy Just To Dance With You' (Lennon)
'And I Love Her' (Lennon)
'Tell Me Why' (Lennon)
'Can't Buy Me Love' (Lennon)
'Any Time At All' (Lennon)
'I'll Cry Instead' (Lennon)
'Things We Said Today' (Lennon)
'When I Get Home' (Lennon)
'You Can't Do That' (Lennon)
'I'll Be Back' (Lennon)

'I Feel Fine' (Lennon)   Single (Nov 1964)
'She's A Woman' (Lennon)   'I Feel Fine' B-side (Nov 1964)

'No Reply' (Lennon)   *Beatles For Sale* (Nov 1964)
'I'm A Loser' (Lennon)
'Baby's In Black' (Lennon)
'I'll Follow The Sun' (Lennon)
'Eight Days A Week' (Lennon)
'Every Little Thing' (Lennon)

'I Don't Want To Spoil The Party' (Lennon)
'What You're Doing' (Lennon)

'Ticket To Ride' (Lennon)   Single (Apr 1965)
'Yes It Is' (Lennon)   'Ticket To Ride' B-side (Apr 1965)

'I'm Down' (Lennon)   'Help!' B-side (Jul 1965)

'Help!' (Lennon)   *Help!* (Aug 1965)
'The Night Before' (Lennon)
'You've Got To Hide Your Love Away' (Lennon)
'Another Girl' (Lennon)
'You're Going To Lose That Girl' (Lennon)
'It's Only Love' (Lennon)
'Tell Me What You See' (Lennon)
'I've Just Seen A Face' (Lennon)
'Yesterday' (Lennon)

'That Means A Lot' (Lennon)   *Anthology 2* (Mar 1996)

'We Can Work It Out' (Lennon)   Single (Dec 1965)
'Day Tripper' (Lennon)   'We Can Work It Out' B-side (Dec 1965)

'Drive My Car' (Lennon)   *Rubber Soul* (Nov 1965)
'Norwegian Wood (This Bird Has Flown)' (Lennon)
'You Won't See Me' (Lennon)
'Nowhere Man' (Lennon)
'The Word' (Lennon)
'Michelle' (Lennon)
'What Goes On' (Lennon-Starkey)
'Girl' (Lennon)
'I'm Looking Through You' (Lennon)
'In My Life' (Lennon)
'Wait' (Lennon)
'Run For Your Life' (Lennon)

'12-Bar Original' (Lennon-Harrison-Starkey)   *Anthology 2* (Mar 1996)

'Paperback Writer' (Lennon)   Single (Jun 1966)
'Rain' (Lennon)   'Paperback Writer' B-side (Jun 1966)

'Eleanor Rigby' (Lennon)	*Revolver* (Aug 1966)
'I'm Only Sleeping' (Lennon)	
'Here, There And Everywhere' (Lennon)	
'Yellow Submarine' (Lennon)	
'She Said She Said' (Lennon)	
'Good Day Sunshine' (Lennon)	
'And Your Bird Can Sing' (Lennon)	
'For No One' (Lennon)	
'Doctor Robert' (Lennon)	
'Got To Get You Into My Life' (Lennon)	
'Tomorrow Never Knows' (Lennon)	
'Penny Lane' (Lennon)	Single (Feb 1967)
'Strawberry Fields Forever' (Lennon)	'Penny Lane' B-side (Feb 1967)
'Sgt Pepper's Lonely Hearts Club Band' (Lennon)	*Sgt Pepper's Lonely Hearts Club Band* (Jun 1967)
'With A Little Help From My Friends' (Lennon)	
'Lucy In The Sky With Diamonds' (Lennon)	
'Getting Better' (Lennon)	
'Fixing A Hole' (Lennon)	
'She's Leaving Home' (Lennon)	
'Being For The Benefit Of Mr Kite!' (Lennon)	
'When I'm Sixty-Four' (Lennon)	
'Lovely Rita' (Lennon)	
'Good Morning Good Morning' (Lennon)	
'Sgt Pepper's Lonely Hearts Club Band (Reprise)' (Lennon)	
'A Day In The Life' (Lennon)	
'All Together Now' (Lennon)	*Yellow Submarine* (Jan 1969)
'All You Need Is Love' (Lennon)	Single (Jul 1967)
'Baby You're A Rich Man' (Lennon)	'All You Need Is Love' B-side (Jul 1967)
'You Know My Name' (Lennon)	'Let It Be' B-side (May 1970)
'Hello Goodbye' (Lennon)	Single (Dec 1967)
'Magical Mystery Tour' (Lennon)	*Magical Mystery Tour* (Dec 1967)
'The Fool On The Hill' (Lennon)	

'Flying' (Lennon-Harrison-Starkey)
'Your Mother Should Know' (Lennon)
'I Am The Walrus' (Lennon)

'Jessie's Dream'   *Magical Mystery Tour* film (Dec 1967)
    (Lennon-Harrison-Starkey)

'Christmas Time (Is Here Again)'   'Free As A Bird' B-side (Dec 1995)
    (Lennon-Harrison-Starkey)

'Lady Madonna' (Lennon)   Single (Mar 1968)

'Hey Jude' (Lennon)   Single (Aug 1968)

'Across The Universe' (Lennon)   *World Wildlife* (Dec 1969)

'Hey Bulldog' (Lennon)   *Yellow Submarine* (Jan 1969)

'Back In The USSR' (Lennon)   *The Beatles* (Nov 1968)
'Dear Prudence' (Lennon)
'Glass Onion' (Lennon)
'Ob-La-Di, Ob-La-Da' (Lennon)
'Honey Pie' (Lennon)
'The Continuing Story Of Bungalow Bill' (Lennon)
'Happiness Is A Warm Gun' (Lennon)
'Martha My Dear' (Lennon)
'I'm So Tired' (Lennon)
'Blackbird' (Lennon)
'Rocky Raccoon' (Lennon)
'Why Don't We Do It In The Road' (Lennon)
'I Will' (Lennon)
'Julia' (Lennon)
'Birthday' (Lennon)
'Yer Blues' (Lennon)
'Mother Nature's Son' (Lennon)
'Everybody's Got Something To Hide Except Me And My Monkey' (Lennon)
'Sexy Sadie' (Lennon)
'Helter Skelter' (Lennon)
'Revolution 1' (Lennon)
'Honey Pie' (Lennon)

'Cry Baby Cry' (Lennon)
'Revolution 9' (Lennon)
'Good Night' (Lennon)

'The Ballad Of John And Yoko' (Lennon)   Single (May 1969)

'Two Of Us' (Lennon)   *Let It Be* (May 1970)
'Dig A Pony' (Lennon)
'Across The Universe' (Lennon)
'I Me Mine' (Harrison [-McCartney?])
'Dig It' (Lennon-Harrison-Starkey)
'Let It Be' (Lennon)
'I've Got A Feeling' (Lennon)
'One After 909' (Lennon)
'The Long And Winding Road' (Lennon)
'Get Back' (Lennon)

'Don't Let Me Down' (Lennon)   'Get Back' B-side (Apr 1969)

'Come Together' (Lennon)   *Abbey Road* (Sep 1969)
'Maxwell's Silver Hammer' (Lennon)
'Oh! Darling' (Lennon)
'I Want You (She's So Heavy)' (Lennon)
'Because' (Lennon)
'You Never Give Me Your Money' (Lennon)
'Sun King' (Lennon)
'Mean Mr Mustard' (Lennon)
'Polythene Pam' (Lennon)
'She Came In Through The Bathroom Window' (Lennon)
'Golden Slumbers' (Lennon)
'Carry That Weight' (Lennon)
'The End' (Lennon)
'Her Majesty' (Lennon)

'Free As A Bird' (Lennon-Harrison-Starkey)   *Anthology 1* (Nov 1995)
'Real Love' (Lennon-Harrison-Starkey)   *Anthology 2* (Mar 1996)

'Thinking Of Linking' (Lennon)   *Anthology DVD* (Apr 2003)

PAUL McCARTNEY

'Family Way' (original soundtrack)	*Family Way* (Feb 1967)
'The Lovely Linda'	*McCartney* (Apr 1970)
'That Would Be Something'	
'Valentine Day'	
'Every Night'	
'Hot As Sun'	
'Glasses'	
'Suicide'	
'Junk'	
'Man We Was Lonely'	
'Oo You'	
'Momma Miss America'	
'Teddy Boy'	
'Maybe I'm Amazed'	
'Kreen Akrore'	
'Another Day' (L McCartney)	Single (Feb 1971)
'Oh Woman, Oh Why'	'Another Day' B-side (Feb 1971)
'Wonderful Christmastime'	Single (Nov 1979)
'Same Time Next Year'	'Put It There' B-side (Feb 1990)
'Coming Up'	*McCartney II* (May 1980)
'Temporary Secretary'	
'On The Way'	
'Waterfalls'	
'Nobody Knows'	
'Front Parlour'	
'Summer's Day Song'	
'Frozen Jap'	
'Bogey Music'	
'Darkroom'	
'One Of These Days'	
'Check My Machine'	'Waterfalls' B-side (Jun 1980)
'Secret Friend'	'Temporary Secretary' B-side (Sep 1980)

'Tug Of War'   *Tug Of War* (Apr 1982)
'Take It Away'
'Always Somebody Who Cares'
'What's That You're Doing' (Wonder)
'Here Today'
'Ballroom Dancing'
'The Pound Is Sinking'
'Wanderlust'
'Get It'
'Be What You See'
'Dress Me Up As A Robber'
'Ebony And Ivory'

'Rainclouds'   'Ebony And Ivory' B-side (Mar 1982)

'I'll Give You A Ring'   'Take It Away' B-side (Jun 1982)

'Pipes Of Peace'   *Pipes Of Peace* (Oct 1983)
'Say Say Say' (Jackson)
'The Other Me'
'Keep Under Cover'
'So Bad'
'The Man' (Jackson)
'Sweetest Little Show'
'Average Person'
'Hey Hey' (Clarke)
'Tug Of Peace'
'Through Our Love'

'Twice In A Lifetime'   *Pipes Of Peace* (Re-released Aug 1993)

'Ode To A Koala Bear'   'Say Say Say' B-side (Oct 1983)

'No More Lonely Nights'   *Give My Regards To Broad Street* (Oct 1984)
'Corridor Music'
'Not Such A Bad Boy'
'No Values'
'Eleanor's Dream'
'Goodnight Princess'

'Stranglehold' (Stewart)	*Press To Play* (Sep 1986)
'Good Times Coming'	
'Talk More Talk'	
'Footprints' (Stewart)	
'Only Love Remains'	
'Press'	
'Pretty Little Head' (Stewart)	
'Move Over Busker' (Stewart)	
'Angry' (Stewart)	
'However Absurd' (Stewart)	
'Write Away' (Stewart)	
'It's Not True'	
'Tough On A Tightrope' (Stewart)	
'Feel The Sun'	
'Hanglide' (Stewart)	'Press' B-side (Jul 1986)
'Simple As That'	*It's A Live-In World* (Nov 1986)
'Spies Like Us'	Single (Nov 1986)
'Love Mix' (Ramone)	'Beautiful Night' B-side (Jul 1997)
'Love Come Tumbling Down'	'Beautiful Night' B-side (Jul 1997)
'Same Love'	'Beautiful Night' B-side (Jul 1997)
'Once Upon A Long Ago'	Single (Nov 1987)
'Back On My Feet' (McManus)	'Once Upon A Long Ago' B-side (Nov 1987)
'Flying To My Home'	'My Brave Face' B-side (May 1989)
'My Brave Face' (McManus)	*Flowers In The Dirt* (Jun 1989)
'Rough Ride'	
'You Want Her Too' (McManus)	
'Distractions'	
'We Got Married'	
'Put It There'	
'Figure Of Eight'	
'This One' (McManus)	
'Don't Be Careless Love' (McManus)	
'That Day Is Done' (McManus)	

'How Many People?'
'Motor Of Love'
'Où Est Le Soleil?'

'I Wanna Cry'	'This One' B-side (Jul 1989)
'The First Stone' (Stewart)	'This One' B-side (Jul 1989)
'Good Sign'	'This One' B-side (Jul 1989)

'Loveliest Thing'   'Figure Of Eight' B-side (Nov 1989)

'Inner City Madness'   *Tripping The Live Fantastic* (Nov 1990)
    (L McCartney-McIntosh-Wickens-Stuart-Whitten)
'Together' (L McCartney-McIntosh-Wickens-Stuart-Whitten)

'All My Trials' (Traditional arr McCartney)   Single (Nov 1990)

'PS Love Me Do' (Lennon)   'Birthday' B-side (Oct 1990)

'I Lost My Little Girl'   *Unplugged* (May 1991)

'War'   *Liverpool Oratorio* (Oct 1991)
'School'
'Crypt'
'Father'
'Wedding'
'Work'
'Crises'
'Peace'

'Off The Ground'   *Off The Ground* (Feb 1993)
'Biker Like An Icon'
'Peace In The Neighbourhood'
'Looking For Changes'
'Hope Of Deliverance'
'Mistress And Maid' (McManus)
'I Owe It All To You'
'Golden Earth Girl'
'The Lovers That Never Were' (McManus)
'Get Out Of My Way'
'Winedark Open Sea'

'C'mon People'
'Cosmically Conscious'

'Style Style'   *Off The Ground* (US release, Apr 1993)
'Sweet Sweet Memories'
'Soggy Noodle'

'Long Leather Coat' (L McCartney) 'Hope Of Deliverance' B-side (Dec 1992)
'Big Boys Bickering'   'Hope Of Deliverance' B-side (Dec 1992)
'Kicked Around No More'   'Hope Of Deliverance' B-side (Dec 1992)

'I Can't Imagine'   'C'mon People' B-side (Feb 1993)
'Keep Coming Back To Love' (Stuart)   'C'mon People' B-side (Feb 1993)
'Down To The River'   'C'mon People' B-side (Feb 1993)

'Hotel In Benidorm'   *Paul Is Live* (Nov 1993)
'A Fine Day'

'Fire/Rain'   *Standing Stone* (Sep 1997)
'Cell Growth'
'Human' Theme
'Meditation'
'Crystal Ship'
'Sea Voyage'
'Lost At Sea'
'Release'
'Safe Haven/Standing Stone'
'Peaceful Moment'
'Messenger'
'Lament'
'Trance'
'Eclipse'
'Glory Tales'
'Fugal Celebration'
'Rustic Dance'
'Love Duet'
'Celebration'

'The Song We Were Singing'   *Flaming Pie* (May 1997)
'The World Tonight'

'If You Wanna'
'Somedays'
'Young Boy'
'Calico Skies'
'Flaming Pie'
'Heaven On A Sunday'
'Used To Be Bad' (Miller)
'Souvenir'
'Little Willow'
'Really Love You' (Starkey)
'Beautiful Night'
'Great Day'

'Oobu Joobu'	'Young Boy' B-side (Apr 1997)
'Broomstick'	'Young Boy' B-side (Apr 1997)
'Atlantic Ocean'	'Young Boy' B-side (Apr 1997)
'I Love This House'	'Young Boy' B-side (Apr 1997)

'Squid'   'The World Tonight' B-side (Jul 1997)

'Run Devil Run'   *Run Devil Run* (Aug 1999)
'Try Not To Cry'
'What It Is'

'A Leaf'   *Working Classical* (Oct 1999)
'Haymakers'
'Midwife'
'Spiral'
'Tuesday'

'From A Lover To A Friend'   *Driving Rain* (Nov 2001)
'Freedom'
'Lonely Road'
'Heather'
'She's Given Up Talking'
'Driving Rain'
'I Do'
'Tiny Bubble'
'Magic'
'Your Way'

'Spinning On An Axis' (J McCartney)
'About You'
'Back In The Sunshine Again' (J McCartney)
'Your Loving Flame'
'Riding Into Jaipur'
'Rinse The Raindrops'

'Vanilla Sky'   *Vanilla Sky* soundtrack (Nov 2001)

PAUL AND LINDA McCARTNEY
'Too Many People'   *Ram* (May 1971)
'Three Legs'
'Ram On'
'Dear Boy' (L McCartney)
'Uncle Albert/Admiral Halsey' (L McCartney)
'Smile Away'
'Heart Of The Country' (L McCartney)
'Monkberry Moon Delight' (L McCartney)
'Eat At Home' (L McCartney)
'Long Haired Lady' (L McCartney)
'Back Seat Of My Car'

PAUL McCARTNEY AND WINGS
'The Mess' (L McCartney)   'My Love' B-side (Mar 1973)

'Big Barn Bed' (L McCartney)   *Red Rose Speedway* (May 1973)
'My Love' (L McCartney)
'Get On The Right Thing' (L McCartney)
'One More Kiss' (L McCartney)
'Little Lamb Dragonfly' (L McCartney)
'Single Pigeon' (L McCartney)
'When The Night' (L McCartney)
'Loup (1st Indian On The Moon)' (L McCartney)
Medley: 'Hold Me Tight/Lazy Dynamite/Hands Of Love/Power Cut'
      (L McCartney)

'Helen Wheels'   Single (Oct 1973)
'Country Dreamer'   'Helen Wheels' B-side (Oct 1973)

'Band On The Run'   *Band On The Run* (Nov 1973)

'Jet'
'Bluebird'
'Mrs Vanderbilt'
'Let Me Roll It'
'Mamunia'
'No Words' (Laine)
'Picasso's Last Words (Drink To Me)'
'1985'

'Zoo Gang'	'Band On The Run' B-side (Jun 1974)

'Junior's Farm'	Single (Oct 1974)
'Sally G'	'Junior's Farm' B-side (Oct 1974)

WINGS

'Mumbo' (L McCartney)	*Wild Life* (Dec 1971)

'Bip Bop' (L McCartney)
'Wild Life' (L McCartney)
'Some People Never Know' (L McCartney)
'I Am Your Singer' (L McCartney)
'Tomorrow' (L McCartney)
'Dear Friend' (L McCartney)

'Give Ireland Back To The Irish' (L McCartney)	Single (Feb 1972)

'Mama's Little Girl'	'Put It There' B-side (Feb 1990)

'Mary Had A Little Lamb' (L McCartney)	Single (May 1972)
'Little Woman Love' (L McCartney)	'Mary Had A Little Lamb' B-side (May 1972)

'C Moon' (L McCartney)	Single (Dec 1972)
'Hi Hi Hi' (L McCartney)	'C Moon' B-side (Dec 1972)

'Live And Let Die' (L McCartney)	Single (Jun 1973)
'I Lie Around' (L McCartney)	'Live And Let Die' B-side (Jun 1973)

'Venus And Mars'	*Venus And Mars* (May 1975)

'Rock Show'
'Love In Song'

'You Gave Me The Answer'
'Magneto And Titanium Man'
'Letting Go'
'Venus And Mars (reprise)'
'Spirits Of Ancient Egypt'
'Call Me Back Again'
'Listen To What The Man Said'
'Treat Her Gently'
'Lonely Old People'

'My Carnival'   *Venus And Mars* (Re-released Oct 1987)

'Lunch Box/Odd Sox'   'Coming Up' B-side (Apr 1980)

'Let 'Em In'   *Wings At The Speed Of Sound* (Mar 1976)
'The Note You Never Wrote'
'She's My Baby'
'Beware My Love'
'Silly Love Songs'
'Cook Of The House' (L McCartney)
'Must Do Something About It'
'San Ferry Anne'
'Warm And Beautiful'

'Soily'   *Wings Over America* (Dec 1976)

'Mull Of Kintyre' (Laine)   Single (Nov 1977)

'Girls' School'   'Mull Of Kintyre' B-side (Nov 1977)

'London Town' (Laine)   *London Town* (Mar 1978)
'Cafe On The Left Bank'
'I'm Carrying'
'Backwards Traveller'
'Cuff Link'
'Children Children' (Laine)
'Girlfriend'
'I've Had Enough'
'With A Little Luck'
'Famous Groupies'

'Deliver Your Children' (Laine)
'Name And Address'
'Don't Let It Bring You Down' (Laine)
'Morse Moose And The Grey Goose' (Laine)
'Waterspout' (bootleg only)

'Daytime Nightime Suffering'   'Goodnight Tonight' B-side (Mar 1979)

'Reception'   *Back To The Egg* (Jun 1979)
'Getting Closer'
'We're Open Tonight'
'Spin It On'
'Old Siam Sir'
'Arrow Through Me'
'Rockestra Theme'
'To You'
'After The Ball/Million Miles'
'Winter Rose/Love Awake'
'The Broadcast'
'So Glad To See You Here'
'Baby's Request'

PAUL McCARTNEY AND THE FROG CHORUS
'We All Stand Together'   Single (Nov 1984)

PAUL McCARTNEY/SUPER FURRY ANIMALS
'Plastic Beetle'   *Liverpool Sound Collage* (Oct 2000)
'Peter Blake 2000'
'Real Gone Dub Made In Manifest In The Vortex Of The Eternal Now'
'Made Up'
'Free Now'

THE FIREMAN
'Transpiritual Stomp' (Youth)   *Strawberries Oceans Ships Forest* (Nov 1993)
'Trans Lunar Rising' (Youth)
'Transcrystaline' (Youth)
'Pure Trance' (Youth)
'Arizona Light' (Youth)
'Celtic Stomp' (Youth)
'Strawberries Oceans Ships Forest' (Youth)

'4 4 4' (Youth)
'Sunrise Mix' (Youth)

'Watercolour Guitars'   *Rushes* (Oct 1998)
'Palo Verde'
'Auraveda'
'Fluid'
'Appletree Cinnabar Amber'
'Bison'
'7am'
'Watercolour Rush'

THE COUNTRY HAMS
'Bridge Over The River Suite' (L McCartney)   Single (Oct 1974)

SUZIE AND THE RED STRIPES
'B-Side To Seaside' (L McCartney)   'Seaside Woman' B-side (Aug 1979)

CHRIS BARBER BAND
'Catcall'   Single (Oct 1967)

CILLA BLACK
'Love Of The loved' (Lennon)   Single (Sep 1963)

'It's For You' (Lennon)   Single (Jul 1964)

'Step Inside Love' (Lennon)   Single (May 1968)

BLACK DYKE MILLS BAND
'Thingumybob' (Lennon)   Single (Aug 1968)

JOHNNY CASH
'New Moon Over Jamaica' (Cash-Hall)   *Water From The Wells*
                                            Of Home (Nov 1988)

JOHN CHRISTIE
'Fourth Of July' (L McCartney)   Single (Jul 1974)

ELVIS COSTELLO
'Pads, Paws And Claws' (McManus)   *Spike* (Feb 1989)
'Veronica' (McManus)

'Playboy To A Man' (McManus)   *Mighty Like A Rose* (May 1991)
'So Like Candy' (McManus)

'Shallow Grave' (McManus)   *All This Useless Beauty* (May 1996)

ROGER DALTREY
'Giddy'   *One Of The Boys* (May 1977)

JOHNNY DEVLIN AND THE DEVILS
'Won't You Be My Baby?' (Devlin)   Aus Single (Feb 1965)

THE EVERLY BROTHERS
'On The Wings Of A Nightingale'   Single (Oct 1984)

THE FOURMOST
'Hello Little Girl' (Lennon)   Single (Aug 1963)

'I'm In Love' (Lennon)   Single (Nov 1963)

ALLEN GINSBERG
'Ballad Of The Skeletons' (Ginsberg-Glass)   Single (Oct 1996)

MARY HOPKIN
'Goodbye' (Lennon)   Single (Mar 1969)

BILLY J KRAMER AND THE DAKOTAS
'Bad To Me' (Lennon)   Single (Jul 1963)

'I'll Keep You Satisfied' (Lennon)   Single (Nov 1963)

'From A Window' (Lennon)   Single (Jul 1964)

DENNY LAINE
'Send Me The Heart' (Laine)   *Japanese Tears* (Dec 1980)

PEGGY LEE
'Let's Love'   *Let's Love* (Oct 1974)

LINDA McCARTNEY
'I Got Up' (L McCartney)   *Wide Prairie* (Oct 1998)
'White Coated Man' (L McCartney-Lane)
'Cow' (L McCartney-Lane)

'Appaloosa' (L McCartney)
'The Light Comes From Within' (L McCartney)

MIKE McGEAR
'Bored As Butterscotch' (McGear-McGough) *Woman* (Apr 1972)

'What Do We Really Know?' *McGear* (Oct 1974)
'Norton' (McGear)
'Leave It'
'Have You Got Problems?' (McGear)
'The Casket' (McGough)
'Sweet Baby' (McGear)
'Rainbow Lady' (McGear)
'Simply Love You' (McGear)
'Giving Grease A Ride' (McGear)
'The Man Who Found God On The Moon' (McGear)

'Dance The Do' (McGear) Single (Jul 1975)

CARLOS MENDES
'Penina' Single (Jul 1969)

ADRIAN MITCHELL
'Hot Pursuit' Unreleased
    (L McCartney-Cunningham-McIntosh-Wickens-Stuart)
'Song In Space' Unreleased
    (L McCartney-Cunningham-McIntosh-Wickens-Stuart)

PETER AND GORDON
'World Without Love' (Lennon) Single (Feb 1964)

'Nobody I Know' (Lennon) Single (May 1964)

'I Don't Want To See You Again' (Lennon) Single (Sep 1964)

'Woman' Single (Feb 1966)

THE PLASTIC ONO BAND
'Give Peace A Chance' (Lennon) Single (Jul 1969)

TOMMY QUICKLY
'Tip Of My Tongue' (Lennon)   Single (Jul 1963)

THE SCAFFOLD
'Ten Years After On Strawberry Jam' (L McCartney)   Single (May 1974)

RINGO STARR
'Six O'Clock' (L McCartney)   *Ringo* (Nov 1973)

'Pure Gold'   *Ringo's Rotogravure* (Sep 1976)

'Private Property'   *Stop And Smell The Roses* (Nov 1981)
'Attention'

'Angel In Disguise' (Starkey)   Unreleased

ROD STEWART
'Mine For Me'   *Smiler* (Sep 1974)

STRANGERS WITH MIKE SHANNON
'One And One Is Two' (Lennon)   Single (May 1964)

10CC
'Code Of Silence' (Stewart)   *Mirror Mirror* (Jun 1985)
'Yvonne's The One' (Stewart)

'Don't Break The Promises' (Stewart-Gouldman)   *Meanwhile* (May 1992)

JOHN WILLIAMS
Theme from *The Honorary Consul*   Single (Dec 1983)